"EXPOSED"

True Black History As It Has Never Been Taught

"The Black Holocaust"

Dr. Romeo L. Taylor, Sr., P.M., D.D., B.B.A.

Second Edition, Revised 2003

Published By
Cable TV Advertising Concepts Ltd.
723 South Casino Center Boulevard
Las Vegas, NV 89101-6716

"EXPOSED"

True Black History
As It Has
Never Been Taught

"The Black Holocaust"

By: Dr. Romeo L. Taylor, Sr. P.M., D.D., B.B.A

Publisher:
Cable TV Advertising Concepts Ltd., Las Vegas, NV

First Printing 1993 Second Printing 2003
Printed in the United States of America

Cover Designed by Dr. Romeo L. Taylor, Sr.

ISBN 0-9639907-1-3

Jet Magazine
February 15, 1982

"The Madonna Connection"

NOTE!

This page was reserved for an article and picture from Jet Magazine dated February 15, 1982 titled "The Madonna Connection".

The picture showed Pope John Paul II standing in front of a shrine praying.

At the top of the shrine, in back of the Pope, was a picture of Black Madonna and Christ Child.

Many people in America, including some Black People, refuse to believe, against all evidence, that Mary the Mother of Jesus was Black. Read the section in the book "Black Mary and Christ Child (page 200).

Johnson Publising Co. turned down our request to use their article and picture

Contents

Message to the World

This book was written to promote racial harmony through education. For centuries the world has been misled about the Black Race. Blacks have been portrayed as having a lower intelligence level then most other races—especially the White race. Consequently, many people around the world, including some Black People, believe those lies due to the absence of facts and information to the contrary. The information in this book is not intended to create hate or hostility towards any race. The material here is to correct history with facts and was selected by a committee. Please read with intelligence instead of emotions.

"Exposed" gives factual evidence that Black People were the creators of civilization and society. Black Egyptians created mathematics, science, astrology, astronomy, medicine, religion, philosophy, art, writing, music, architecture, engineering, government, mining, and virtually all other fields involving the elements of civilization. In mathematics, the ancient Egyptians not only developed arithmetic, but also algebra, geometry, trigonometry and calculus.

Today many Egyptians claim to be White. However, Cheikh Anta Diop, a Senegalese professor and scientist claims, "The original ancient Egypt was built by Black Africans long before Egypt was invaded by Assyrians, Libyans, Persians, Greeks, Romans, and Arabs."

At a Cairo symposium in 1974 of the UNESCO Organization, Cheikh Anta Diop, using a 7-point presentation, proved the ancient Egyptians were Black Africans. Even though this was proved, most Egyptians still identify themselves as White. If you are truly interested in Black history, Please read "BLACK PEOPLE & THEIR PLACE IN WORLD HISTORY" and "THE BLACK BOOK." By reading and sharing the information contained in the books we recommend, your children and their children will learn some of the truth about their ancestors.

Those of us involved in this book chose to consider ourselves to be a part of the Black Race for our racial identity. We will not let anyone cut us off from our rich African heritage. Further, members of the White race born in Africa and moved to America, or whose ancestors come from Africa, are African Americans. So we choose to distinguish ourselves by using the complete term of our heritage, "Black African Americans." We don't feel the children of our African oppressors should be entitled to any benefits owed to Black People. At times we may use the terms "Black" or "African American," but be assured we are talking about Black African Americans.

"Genetic Evidence Points to African Origin of Humans"

Reuters: March 31, 1997

* * * * *

Since the overthrow of Egypt by the Romans, evidence of Black Egyptian knowledge has been stolen, destroyed and historically hidden. During the time when Africans were being captured or sold to captors, full operating cities and countries existed and were run by governments of educated Black People. However, the captors have promoted Africans as being savages, ignorant and using any and all other demeaning names they could call them.

This book is written to correct existing information and to support it with factual information in a succinct manner for world consumption. The United States was built by forced, free, Black labor for over 400 years. In developing the United States, Blacks paid with their lives by being lynched, burned at the stake, babies and children used as alligator bait, women, girls and boys raped; flogged to death. Families were separated and language denied; everything that could be done to enslave and destroy a race of people. A tacit, and not so tacit, form of genocide.

The Jews want the world to remember the Jewish Holocaust. They say never again. However, the United States wants to forget about the Black Holocaust.

We Also Say "NEVER AGAIN"

This book should be considered as a Black History Reference Book, referring you to books where further details can be found concerning the information used in this book.

A lot of the information in this book, was copyrighted in the 1940's and 1950's, and has remained available to the public.

Also, the books we have used only touch the surface in telling the true story of the contributions to mankind by Black People. There are hundreds of books dedicated to exposing the truth. We have only selected a few, hoping we can stimulate enough interest to cause people to search further. We encourage you to read the books and other information to which we refer you. We also encourage others with information to write books, as well.

There are graphic pictures and descriptions of acts committed against Blacks. These are a part of American history and should demonstrate the suffering endured by Black People. No other race in this country has had to endure the atrocities that Blacks survived and are continually confronted with in their daily life.

The use of the term White people is only to identify the race of the people involved (e.g., when a crime is committed in this country, they identify the race if the crime was committed by a Black or Hispanic person. If the crime was committed by a White person, they don't identify the race as White).

Acknowledgements

We would like to thank the thousands of people that participated in our surveys and contributed their views and information to this book including, but not limited to the following:

Tom Green
Carol Wilson
Harold Brown
Ella Love
Buddy Jones
Dr. Henry Ajie
Dr. Leroy William Vaughn
Prince Hall Masons
Mr. John Peoples, "Peoples Helping our People"
Ted Terry
Brother Cliff Pruette
Carolynne Banks
Big Money Griff (Morris Griffin)
B. Hall
Shaba Shabaka
Trena Garner
Jean Reece
Fitzgerald Othello
Ann Overton
Dr. Creasie Page
Dorothy Thornton
Juanita Davis
Charles Dauzat
Henry Davis

Thanks to God

I give thanks to God
For the many blessings He has bestowed upon me.

I give thanks to God
For leading me down the path in life that
He has directed me.

I give thanks to God
For giving me the ability to utilize the information
He has supplied to me.

I give thanks to God
For the many people
He has sent my way, to help complete this book.

I give thanks to God
For allowing us to share this information
With the world.

I only ask You, God, to
Open the hearts and minds of our people and

Let them read with intelligence instead of emotions.

Let them know that they are Your children, and The
truth can set them free; if they accept it.

Thank You, God,
Dr. Romeo L. Taylor, Sr.

Dedication

This book is dedicated to the ancestors of all Black People all over the world.

To those Black People who suffered and died without their stories being told.

To the millions of Black People that were forced to work relentlessly in the fields and factories, building this nation and making it rich; without being compensated.

To other races of the world, after reading this book, you should finally give respect to Black People. It is long overdue.

To Black People all over the world, that have lost hope due to centuries of brain washing, you should lift up your heads, stick out your chest and say,

"I Am Somebody."

I come from the Creators of Civilization, of Arts and Sciences, from inventors that made life better for all mankind,

"I Am Somebody."

To all the Black People that dream dreams, but failed to act upon their dreams.

"IT'S NEVER TOO LATE"

Dr. Romeo L. Taylor, Sr.
Hotep (peace)

Special Recognition

Thanks to my daughter, Dominga Taylor Hill, for her continuing support and encouragement. She was there when no one else was. May this book elevate her life.

* * * * *

Special Recognition of Writers

Some material in this book has been taken from the following writers. We feel they deserve "Special Recognition" for their contributions to Black awareness and encourage you to read their books. We have only touched the surface. There are many more writers with equal qualifications that have written material containing information as important as the information contained herein.

J.A. Rogers

J.A. Rogers spent more than fifty years in anthropological and historical research on the Negro in all ages and all lands. He traveled extensively, particularly in Europe and Africa. He was present at the coronation of Haile Selassie I, in 1930 and was a newspaper correspondent in the Italo-Ethiopian War of 1935-36. J.A. Rogers received a gold medal directly from Emperor Haile Selassie of Ethiopia.

J.A. Rogers was a student of race relations, particularly as it effects the broader field of international politics. In 1930 he was elected to membership in the Pam's Society of Anthropology which was founded in 1859. The same year, he was a speaker at the International Congress of Anthropology, which was opened by Payl Doumer, President of France. The Dr. W.E. DuBois stated, "No man living has revealed so many important facts about the Negro as Rogers." His knowledge of world history is more extensive than that of Negro history. Books used as references are listed under List of Sources. We strongly suggest you read all of J.A. Rogers' books.

Rudolph R. Windsor

Rudolph R. Windsor, attended community college in Philadelphia, studying psychology and political science, Grate College, where he majored in Hebraic Studies, and Temple University, where he majored in Middle Eastern Studies. In 1978 he received his B.H.L. degree.

Professor Windsor is a strong advocator of the economic and cultural development of the Black community. In serving the community he has been a member and president of several organizations; was a delegate to the Black Power Conference of 1968 and was designated a delegate, on behalf of Ethiopian Mission, to the United Nations in the early 1970's. Books used as references are listed under List of Sources.

Indus Khamit Kush

Indus Khamit Kush has a B. A. degree from City University (Herbert H. Nehman) and a Masters in

Teaching from Fordham University. Having taught mathematics for 12 years, he has written three math books. At the time this book was written, Indus Khamit Kush was teaching mathematics in a junior college in the Bronx. Books used as reference are listed under List of Sources.

John G. Jackson

John G. Jackson is recognized as an eminent scholar and historian, "Ethiopia and the Origin of Civilization" was first published in 1939. Book used as reference is listed under List of Sources.

William Mosley

William Mosley is a scholar, former pastor and investigator with the Equal Employment Opportunity Commission. He studied at the Moody Bible Institute, and earned a Bachelors and Masters Degree at the University of California, Santa Barbara in Black and Religious Studies. The book used as reference is listed under List of Sources.

Dr. John Henrik Clarke

Dr. John Henrik Clarke became a noted professor of African Studies at several universities including Hunter College and Cornell University. He founded the African and Puerto Rican Studies Departments at Hunter College. His program became the model for all Latino Studies Departments around the country.

Dr. John Henrik Clarke wrote and edited over 30 books, which included many volumes on Africa. A documentary was written and produced about the life of Dr. Clarke, titled the "GREAT AND MIGHTY WALK." This was one of many honors bestowed upon him. Material used as reference is listed under List of Sources.

Dr. Auset BaKhufu

With advanced degrees in sociology and psychology, Auset BaKhufu is a sociologist, psychologist, lecturer, teacher, and writer. She has studied extensively under Dr. John Henrik Clarke, and is a student of herbal remedies and healings, as well as ourstory (history). She says that the healer of the mind and body constitutes the study of Sakku, which is Ancient African Psychology and Philosophy. Dr. BaKhufu is hard at work on her next book project entitled "A DJAMBALYA OF WRITINGS: SOCIETY, BLACK CREATIVITY, AND THE GENESIS AND GENIUS OF WRITING." Also, look for her upcoming fiction authored under the name of Auset Barber. The book, "THE SIX BLACK PRESIDENTS: BLACK BLOOD, WHITE MASKS - USA," is used as a reference here and is listed under the List of Sources.

Dr. Chancellor Williams

Dr. Chancellor Williams received a doctorate in history and sociology. He studied psychology, anthropology, archeology and economics. He also taught Arabic history and worked as a professor of history at Howard University for twenty-nine years. He won an award from the Black Academy of Arts and Letters and was the first recipient of the Twenty-First Century Foundation's Clarence L. Holt prize for excellence in literature. Dr. Williams spent 16 years researching and writing his book, "THE DESTRUCTION OF BLACK CIVILIZATION." The book used as reference is listed under List of Sources.

Dr. Leroy William Vaughn, M.D., M.B.A.

Dr. Leroy William Vaughn was rooted and grounded in Black History as a student at Morehouse College in Atlanta, Georgia where he obtained a Bachelor of Science degree and graduated Phi Beta Kappa in 1969. Dr. Vaughn received the Franklin C. McLean Award in 1972 as the most outstanding Black medical student in the nation. His book "BLACK PEOPLE & THEIR PLACE IN WORLD HISTORY" is a book you must read. Book used as reference is listed under List of Sources.

Dr. Carter Goodwin Woodson

Dr. Carter G. Woodson was an African American historian and educator, and was the founder of the Association for the Study of Negro Life and History. He was the author of more than 16 books, and the founder and editor of the Journal of Negro History and the Negro History Bulletin. His book, "THE MIS-EDUCATION OF THE NEGRO," should be read by everyone. Book used as reference is listed under List of Sources.

* * * * *

INTRODUCTION

"Before European History There Was Black History"

"It is pretty well settled that the city is the Negro's great contribution to civilization, for it was where the first cities grew up."

Haldman-Julius

Read: "ETHIOPIA AND THE ORIGIN OF CIVILIATION

* * * * *

Dr. John Henrik Clark often defined the reason we should study our history with this well-known quote:

"History is a clock that people use to tell their political and cultural time of day. It is also a compass that people use to find themselves on the map of human geography. The role of history is to tell a people what they have been and where they have been. What they are, and where they are. The most important role that history plays is that it has the function of telling a people where they must still go and what they must still be."

* * * * *

Historian Carter G. Woodson states:

"If a race has no history, if it has no worthwhile tradition, it becomes a negligible factor in the thought of the world, and it stands in danger of being exterminated."

THEY SAY

They say, "Knowledge is Power"

By: Jean-Paul Sartre

I SAY,

"Knowledge Shared and Applied is Power !
Knowledge Not Shared Nor Applied, Is Wasted."

By: Dr. Romeo L. Taylor, Sr.

SHARE THIS BOOK AND INFORMATION WITH EVERYONE YOU KNOW

Black History in America, is American History. However if you want to study about Blacks in America it should be American History as it relates to Black People. Throughout history many Black leaders have been manipulated into doing things that are not in the best interest of our race.

The writers of America History neglected to include Black contributions by Blacks in the development of the United States and the world in their history books. They also manipulated some educators to divide American History into Black and White; whereby they didn't have to teach Black involvement in American History.

It worked. Integration became a method of indoctrinating non-Whites into the White culture and history. There was no mention of Black contributions to history. When White schools taught about Africa, they only talked about a land of savages. Busing was to be a tool whereby children studying together would learn more about each other. However, busing, in most cases, only went one way—from the Black community to the White schools. Seldom could you find White students bused into Black schools.

Those busing Black students were only taught about White culture and history. They were not taught African history or culture.

It has been the practice of the people in power to hide, destroy or even change evidence that may relate to facts in this book. The readers should be aware of these practices. Where the evidence or facts have been changed or altered (as with the Black Stature of Liberty), use common sense.

Dr. John Henrik Clarke, often said:

> "Not only had the White man colonized Afrika and its people, he has colonized information about Afrika and its diverse people! In order to maintain White supremacy, the White man has had to constantly distort and lie about history; especially Afrikan and European history.
>
> "The White man knew that if the Truth were ever fully revealed, the myth of White supremacy would crumble into dust."

* * * * *

"Inferiority" is a myth spread by White bigots.
By Carl T. Rowan

* * * * *

TRUTH

"HOW CAN ONE DETERMINE THE TRUTH
WHEN THE CONSPIRACY
IS TO PROMOTE UNTRUTHS ?"

By Dr. Romeo L. Taylor, Sr.

REALITY

"MANS CHOICE TO BELIEVE OR NOT,
ACCEPT OR NOT, DOES NOT CHANGE
THE REALITY OF ANYTHING IN THE UNIVERSE!"
"FACTS ARE FACTS, WHETHER YOU
BELIEVE THEM OR NOT"

By: Dr. Romeo L. Taylor, Sr.

History Written by People in Power

Throughout history, people in power have written history according to their perspective and the way they wanted history to be told. As time goes on, the truth comes out.

American history books were not written for Blacks. They were written from a European perspective, giving inaccurate accounts of history as it relates to the world and the United States. Read:"STOLEN LEGACY" by E.N. James and "BLACK ATHENA" by Martin Bernal.

Each book exposes Greek knowledge as knowledge stolen from the Egyptian Mystery System.

* * * * *

Black children that attend White schools are being taught to adopt a White culture. They teach everything about White culture and history. As these children grow up and remain in this system, they become easy prey to the White racists that want them to reject their cultural identity and assimilate into the White culture and society.

As one Baldwin Hills, California resident said in the March 13, 1989 issue of Time Magazine, "We're a typical White middle class family that happens to be Black." Remember the teachings of Willie Lynch. This was a part of his program, to make some Blacks feel better than others.

* * * * *

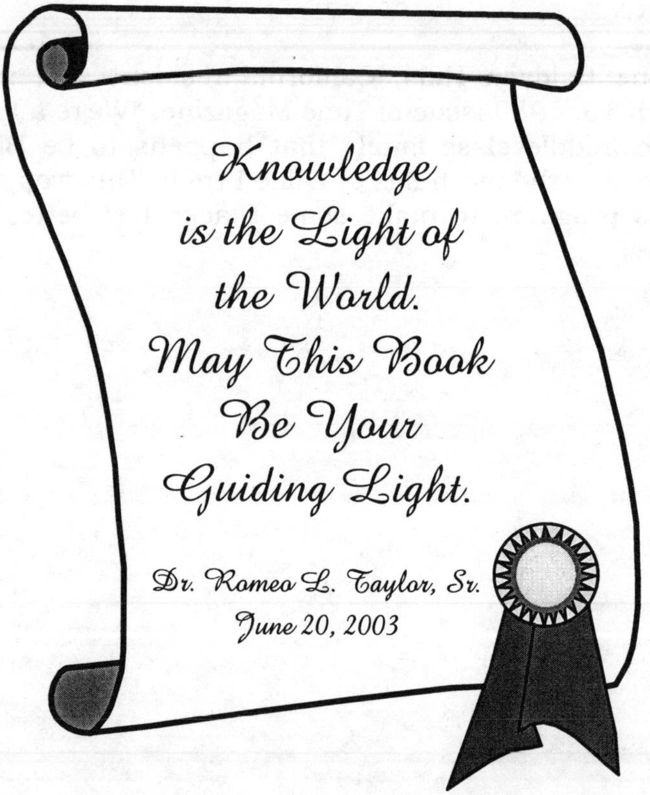
Knowledge
is the Light of
the World.
May This Book
Be Your
Guiding Light.
Dr. Romeo L. Taylor, Sr.
June 20, 2003

Chapter 1

WHO ARE NIGRITIANS ?

Until 146 B.C. Nigritia was the name, given to the land now called Africa.

Negest Shaba Shabaka says,

> "Africa was first applied to the neighborhood of Carthage, the part first known to the Romans. Carthage was part of the empire of Hamilcar and was passed on to his son, Hannibal. The Carthaginian empire extended into the West African coast into what we call today Senegal and Guinea and to Maderia and the Canary Islands.
> "After the third Punic War, which lasted three years, Carthage fell to the Romans. It is said that the Roman general Scipio returned to Carthage with his army and friends. After hard and long resistance the city fell in 146 B.C. The Romans destroyed the city, enslaved the survivors and established the province of Africa. Prior to this time in history, according to ancient maps dated as early as 500 B.C. the entire continent had been called "Nigritia." The people in power have tried to wipe the words "Nigritia" from the face of the world. See the map of 1808 attached. Long before history began to be written, Nigritians had migrated around the globe. Nigritian means "the people from the source" or "the original people."
>
> "In Central and West Africa there are two nations who proudly proclaim themselves to be Nigritic people. The fact is the descendants of ancient

Nigritic people are currently found all over this planet."

SOCIAL HISTORY

OF THE

RACES OF MANKIND.

FIRST DIVISION:

NIGRITIANS.

BY

A. FEATHERMAN.

"Itaque etiam non assecutus, voluisse abunde pulchrum atque magnificum est."

—*Pliny.*

LONDON:
TRÜBNER & CO., LUDGATE HILL.
1885.
[*All rights reserved.*]

Book Published in 1885

Dr. William Smith, another great historian of Egyptian history and culture has examined the language of the ancient Egyptian people. His research into Egyptian and

Nigritian history, and culture is found in a four volume set called "SMITH'S DICTIONARY OF THE BIBLE, VOLUME I, II, III and IV." According to Dr. Smith, "The ancient Egyptian language is one of the dialects of the great Nigritian family of languages."

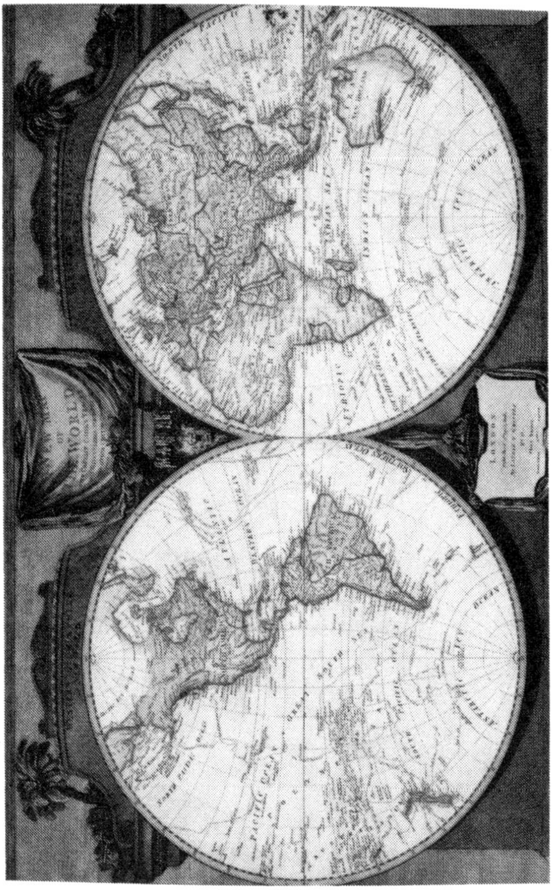

World Map 1808

For more information please read:

"NIGGER, A DIVINE ORIGIN"
by Negest Shaba Shabaka
With Special Linguistic Consulting Services of
Dr. Ernie A. Smith

* * * * *

In Gerald Massey's book, "BOOK OF THE BEGINNING, VOLUME I," he states:

> "Ancient Egyptian language is the ancient Nigritian language."

* * * * *

Chapter 2

WERE BLACKS SLAVES OR CAPTIVES ?

As mentioned before, people of power control communications and the flow of information. They also print dictionaries and determine word definitions. As an example of altering the meaning of a word, the word picnic, according to Funk and Wagnall's, means "An outdoor social outing for which food is usually provided by the people participating."

When in fact, **the word picnic appears to have originated from "pick-a-nigger." Every weekend during the days Blacks were enslaved, mostly in the Southern states, and for many years thereafter, some White people would pick-a-nigger to hang or burn at a stake. This was their weekly party. Sometimes after the hanging or burning, parts of the body were sold as souvenirs.** See pictures in Affirmative Action.

* * * * *

Definitions

We want to deal with two words:

"SLAVE" and "CAPTIVE"

Funk and Wagnall's Standard Encyclopedic Dictionary defines:

"Slave"

1. A person over whose life, liberty and property someone else has absolute control.

2. A person in mental or moral subjection to a habit, vice or influence.

"Captive"

1. One who or that which is captured and held in confinement; a prisoner.

American soldiers captured in the Korea or Vietnam War were made to work for their captors; are they considered slaves? They were captured at one location and taken to another. The title of "CAPTIVE" is the true position of those Africans that were captured and taken from their homes. The captors attempted to enslave them.

"You May Have Control of a Person's Body,
But You Cannot Control Their Mind."
By: Dr. Romeo L. Taylor, Sr.

Therefore, we feel the definition of slave should be:

"Slave"

1. A person who accepts the position of being physically and mentally owned by another person.

The majority of captives did not accept being enslaved

* * * * *

Black Captive Revolts

The following is a time-line of Major Revolts and Escapes before the Emancipation Proclamation.

1526 First recorded captives revolt in North America. First Africans brought to the Carolinas escape to Indian communities.

1663 In Virginia a captive revolt by Black captives and White indentured servants was stopped when a servant exposed the conspiracy

1708 Captives rise up in Long Island.

1712 A captive revolt in New York City, leaving 9 Whites dead, and approximately 20 captives are killed or committed suicide.

1723 Captives burn several plantations and White owned properties in Massachusetts.

1730 In Norfolk and Princess Anne Counties, Virginia, a captive revolt was planned, but was discovered and stopped.

1739 South Carolina had three captive revolts. Dozens of captives and Whites are killed. In the Stono Rebellion, led by a captive named Cato, 30 Whites were killed.

1741 Although there is no evidence that captives were involved in a New York City revolt. 11 captives are burned at the stake, 18 were hanged, and 70 are sold into slavery.

1750 In Framingham, Massachusetts, Crispus Attacks escapes from his captor. He was one of the first colonials killed in the Boston Massacre in 1770.

1782 About 5,000 captives escape from America on British ships leaving Savannah.

1791 A captive revolt in Louisiana resulted in the execution of 23 captives and the exile of three White sympathizers.

1791 In the northern province of Haiti, a revolution was started by captives.

1800 Gabriel Prosser and about 1,000 Captives planned a revolt to take over the capitol of Richmond, Virginia. Prosser and his followers were executed.

1803 In New York City, protesting captives burn houses and riot for several days. Many were arrested and convicted.

1804 Underground Railroad establishes network for runaway captives.

1811 Several hundred captives revolted in Louisiana, not far from New Orleans. Federal and State Troops crush the revolt.

1815 In Florida 300 fugitive captives, turned farmers from Georgia, and 30 Creek Indians seize the former British Fort Blount and create an asylum for runaway captives.

Within a year, U.S. troops destroyed the strong hold, killing about 270 former captives.

1816 Three hundred fugitive slaves and about 20 Indian allies held Fort Blount on Apalachicola Bay, Florida, for several days before it was attacked by U.S. Troops.

1818 Blacks and Seminole Indians battle Andrew Jackson at Suwanee.

1822 Denmark Vesey, a former captive in Charleston, South Carolina, planned an insurrection to seize arsenals, guardhouses, and munitions supplies, and to take the city and kill all Whites. A captive informed on the plans and the plot was foiled. The rebels were arrested; Vesey and 34 others are executed.

1829 Race riot in Cincinnati, Ohio on August 10, 1929. More than 1,000 Negroes left the city for Canada.

1831 Nat Turner Revolt, Southampton County, Virginia, August 21-22, 1831. Some 60 Whites were killed.

Nat Turner was not captured until October 30, 1831. Nat Turner was hanged in Jerusalem, Virginia, on November 11, 1831.

1835 After 8 years of fighting, 500 fugitive captives living with the Seminole Indians were re-enslaved.

1837 John Horse, a Black commander of the Seminole Indians, help defeat U.S. troops at the Battle of Okeechobee in Florida.

1838 Frederick Douglass escaped from slavery in Baltimore, September 3. He changed his name to Frederick Augustus Washington.

1839 Africans led by Cinque revolted aboard the ship La Amistad.

1841 Captive revolt on slave trader ship "Creole" which was enroute to New Orleans, Louisiana. Captives overpowered crew and sailed vessel to Bahamas to freedom.

1848 Ellen Craft posed as a slave owner and her husband, William, acted as her servant, as they escape to freedom.

1849 Harriet Tubman escapes from slavery and assist more than 300 captives in their escape to freedom.

1851 Blacks attack a group of slave-catchers in Pennsylvania.

1859 Blacks join John Brown in raid on Harper's Ferry, a United States arsenal.

1860 Blacks form volunteer troops to fight Confederate Army.

* * * * *

Throughout the period of captivity, many small groups escaped from their captors, but were not recorded.

For more information read:

"BEFORE THE MAYFLOWER" by Lerone Bennett

"TIMELINES OF AFRICAN-AMERICAN HISTORY"

Also, go to:

www.afroam.org/history/slavery/revolts.html

For too long, Americans, both Blacks and Whites, have accepted whatever has been told to them, without question.

* * * * *

Chapter 3

AFFIRMATIVE ACTION

Part Payment for Past Atrocities

When a Black person speaks out about racial injustice, discrimination, past atrocities or anything that is upsetting to the White community, that Black person is branded a militant, troublemaker and / or racist -- even when the facts are clearly in favor of the Black person.

Affirmative Action was originally offered as part payment for past atrocities against Black People. However, the United States government would not pass a bill unless it included other minority races and women. There are some Black People who don't recall where they come from. They feel they made it in life on their own efforts and Affirmative Action is not necessary. They need to read this book and realize that if their ancestors had not died for them, they might very well be enslaved today. Further, there are Black People who try to climb the corporate ladder and put distance between themselves and the Black community. They have not studied history and found that, when the White structure has used you up, you are put back in your place. If everyone else got paid for wrong doings this government did against them; why can't we?

NO OTHER RACE IN THIS COUNTRY PAID THE PRICE FOR PREFERENTIAL TREAMENT LIKE THE BLACK RACE. WE HAVE EARNED EVERYTHING WE ASK FOR, AND MORE.

Let it be known . . .

THE AFFIRMATIVE ACTION PROGRAM IS NOT A GIFT. BLACK PEOPLE PAID WITH THEIR LIVES AND FREE LABOR FOR PREFERENTIAL CONSIDERATION

Now It's Time To Get Compensated

The Affirmative Action Program also recognized the fact that discrimination still existed in education, housing and many employers still use discriminatory practices in hiring. I was listening to a radio news item on January 21, 2003, which stated that persons submitting applications for jobs, etc., with Black or African sounding names, were not considered for most positions. Their applications are trashed.

The Affirmative Action Program set aside 20% out of 100% for minorities. That's two (2) out of every ten (10). Eight (8) are available to Whites, two (2) available to minorities.

Now Whites are crying "reverse discrimination" saying, "The most qualified should get the job."

We agree. But what happens when all are equally qualified? There are 80 White applications and 20 Black. With equal qualifications how does a Black person get consideration, when they are out numbered 8 to 2? Let's stop playing games. For hundreds of years, Whites have been getting jobs where Blacks were not even allowed to put in applications or to be considered for the position.

White society does not believe in quotas. Eighty percent (80%) is not enough for them. They must have 100%! Isn't 80% a quota? Many White people ask, "Why do these people riot? What more do they want?"

What we want is fairness, recognition for our contributions, respect and compensation for work performed.

A recent news report stated, "In a survey it was reported that most Americans oppose Affirmative Action Programs." The problem with that survey is most of those surveyed had not lost one drop of blood in building this nation; nor had their ancestors. The benefits they receive today are from the backs of free Black labor.

Using Numbers As An Example

Three thousand students apply for entrance to a university. There are 2,000 seats available. The population of the United States is 12.7% Black. Perhaps 25% are of college age and 15% apply. Therefore 57 Blacks place an application; while 2,943 Whites and others, place applications. With all being equally qualified and only 2,000 slots available, how will the Black students get accepted?

Other races come here and enjoy the "American Dream," which would not be so enjoyable without the inventions of Black People. We don't hold other races responsible for their concept of Black People because they only react to what they have been taught prior to coming here. However, common sense should be used by all people. By looking around, anyone can see Blacks are not mentally inferior in any way.

* * * * *

"White Privilege Shapes the U.S."

by Robert Jensen

Here is what White Privilege sounds like:

I am sitting in my University of Texas office, talking to a very bright and very conservative White student about affirmative action in college admissions, which he opposes and I support.

The student says he wants a level playing field with no unearned advantages for anyone. I ask him whether he thinks that in the United States being White has advantages. Have either of us, I ask, ever benefited from being White in a world run mostly by White people? Yes, he concedes, there is something real and tangible we could call White privilege.

So, if we live in a world of White privilege – unearned White privilege – how does that affect your notion of a level playing field? I ask.

He paused for a moment and said, "That really doesn't matter."

That statement, I suggested to him, reveals the

ultimate White privilege: the privilege to acknowledge you have unearned privilege but ignore what it means.

That exchange led me to rethink the way I talk about race and racism with students. It drove home to me the importance of confronting the dirty secret that we White people carry around with us everyday: In a world of White privilege, some of what we have is unearned. I think much of both the fear and anger that comes up around discussions of affirmative action has its roots in that secret. So these days, my goal is to talk openly and honestly about White supremacy and White privilege.

White privilege, like any social phenomenon, is complex. In a White supremacist culture, all White people have privilege, whether or not they are overtly racist themselves. There are general patterns, but such privilege plays out differently depending on context and other aspects of one's identity (in case, being male gives me other kinds of privilege). Rather than try to tell others how White privilege has played out in their lives, I talk about how it has affected me.

I am as White as White gets in this country. I am of northern European heritage and I was raised in North Dakota, one of the Whitest states in the country. I grew up in a virtually all-White world surrounded by racism, both personal and institutional. Because I didn't live near a reservation, I didn't even have exposure to the state's only numerically significant non-White population, American Indians.

I have struggled to resist that racist training and the ongoing racism of my culture. I like to think I have changed, even though I routinely trip over the lingering effects of that internalized racism and the institutional racism around me. But no matter how much I "fix" myself, one thing never changes – I walk through the world with White privilege.

What does that mean? Perhaps most importantly, when I seek admission to a university, apply for a job, or hunt for an apartment, I don't look threatening. Almost all of the people evaluating me for those things look like me – they are White. They see in me a reflection of themselves, and in a racist world that is an advantage. I smile, I am White. I am one of them. I am not dangerous. Even when I voice critical opinions, I am cut some slack. After all, I'm White.

My flaws also are more easily forgiven because I am White. Some complain that affirmative action has meant the university is saddled with mediocre minority professors. I have no doubt there are minority faculty who are mediocre, though I don't know very many. As Henry Louis Gates, Jr. once pointed out, if affirmative action policies were in place for the next hundred years, it's possible that at the end of that time the university could have as many mediocre minority professors as it has mediocre White professors. That isn't meant as an insult to anyone, but is a simple observation that White privilege has meant that scores of second-rate White professors have slid through the system because their flaws were overlooked out of solidarity based on race, as well as on gender, class and ideology.

Some people resist the assertions that the United States is still a bitterly racist society and that the racism has real effects on real people. But White folks have long cut other White folks a break. I know, because I am one of them.

I am not a genius—as I like to say, I'm not the sharpest knife in the drawer. I have been teaching full-time for six years, and I've published a reasonable amount of scholarship. Some of it is the unexceptional stuff one churns out to get tenure, and some of it, I would argue, actually is worth reading. I work hard, and I like to think that I'm a fairly decent teacher. Every once in awhile, I leave my office at the end of the day feeling like I really accomplished something. When I cash my paycheck, I don't feel guilty.

But, all that said, I know I did not get where I am by merit alone. I benefited from, among other things, White privilege. That doesn't mean that I don't deserve my job, or that if I weren't White I would never have gotten the job. It means simply that all through my life, I have soaked up benefits for being White. I grew up in fertile farm country taken by force from non-White indigenous people. I was educated in a well-funded, virtually all-White public school system in which I learned that White people like me made this country great. There I also was taught a variety of skills, including how to take standardized tests written by and for White people.

All my life I have been hired for jobs by White

people. I was accepted for graduate school by White people. I was hired for a teaching position at the predominantly White University of Texas, which had a White president, in college headed by a White dean and in a department with a White chairman that at the time had one non-White tenured professor.

There certainly is individual variation in experience. Some White people have had it easier than me, probably because they came from wealthy families that gave them even more privilege. Some White people have had it tougher than me because they came from poorer families. White women face discrimination I will never know. But in the end, White people all have drawn on White privilege somewhere in their lives.

Like anyone, I have overcome certain hardships in my life. I have worked hard to get where I am, and I work hard to stay there. But to feel good about myself and my work, I do not have to believe that "merit," as defined by White people in a White country, alone got me here. I can acknowledge that in addition to all that hard work, I got a significant boost from White privilege, which continues to protect me every day of my life from certain hardships.

At one time in my life, I would not have been able to say that, because I needed to believe that my success in life was due solely to my individual talent and effort. I saw myself as the heroic American, the rugged individualist. I was so deeply seduced by the culture's mythology that I couldn't see the fear that was binding me to those myths. Like all White Americans, I was living with the fear that maybe I didn't really deserve my success, that maybe luck and privilege had more to do with it than brains and hard work I was afraid I wasn't heroic or rugged, that I wasn't special.

I lct go of some of that fear when I realized that, indeed, I wasn't special, but that I was still me. What I do well, I still can take pride in, even when I know that the rules under which I work in are stacked in my benefit. I believe that until we let go of the fiction that people have complete control over their fate, that we can will ourselves to be anything we choose, then we will live with that fear. Yes, we should all dream big and pursue our dreams and not let anyone or anything stop us. But we all are the product, both of what we will ourselves to be and what the society in which we live lets us be.

White privilege is not something I get to decide whether or not I want to keep. Every time I walk into a store at the same time as a black man and the security guard follows him and leaves me alone to shop, I am benefiting from White privilege. There is not space here to list all the ways in which White privilege plays out in our daily lives, but it is clear that I will carry this privilege with me until the day White supremacy is erased from this society.

Frankly, I don't think I will live to see that day; I am realistic about the scope of the task. However, I continue to have hope, to believe in the creative power of human beings to engage the world honestly and act morally. A first step for White people, I think, is to not be afraid to admit that we have benefited from White privilege. It doesn't mean we are frauds who have no claim to our success. It means we face a choice about what we do with our success.

By Robert Jenson

Robert Jensen is a Professor in the Department of Journalism at the University of Texas at Austin.
rjensen@uts.ccutexas.edu

Statistics on White vs. Black

During the writing of the first edition of this book, we received some interesting information:

The media insists that Black People are the recipients of special treatment and that African Americans are on a par with Whites today. This is untrue.

Newsweek Magazine 1993, Affirmative Action

Drugs in Black and White,
Crime / Violence;
Welfare / Poverty / Illegitimacy; Genetics.

According to the March 29, 1993 issue of Newsweek Magazine, White males make up 39% of the population, yet they account for the following:

1. 82.5% of the Forbes 400
   (People with at least $265 million)

2. 77% of the Congressmen
3. 92% of State Governors

4. 70% of tenured college faculty

5. 90% of daily newspaper editions

6. 77% of television and newspapers

7. They head virtually all of the major corporations

8. They have the highest employment rate in the nation

9. Even in the NBA, most of the head coaches and general managers are White males

Drugs

According to Robert DuPont, former director of the National Institute of Drug Abuse, 80% of America's drug abusers are White and only 14% are Black.

According to a New York Times survey, the typical crack addict is a 40-year old White male professional, married and suburban.

According to Dr. Arnold Washington, director of a New York treatment center, there are more crack addicts among the White middle class than in any other segment of the population.

According to the Children's Defense Fund, White women have the highest percentage of cocaine pregnancies.

Drugs in Black and White

Atlanta Television 1990

Parents Resource Institute for Drug Education (P.R.I.D.E) -- 400,000 High School Seniors and Juniors were surveyed:

Cocaine Use	1.5%	Black	4.7%	White
Marijuana Use	8.4%	Black	21.2%	White
Liquor Use	15.3%	Black	51.6%	White

National Institute of Drug Abuse Household Survey

43%	More Whites than Blacks used marijuana
129%	More Whites than Blacks used cocaine
70%	More Whites than Blacks used alcohol

The leading cause of death among American teenagers is automobile accidents; over half of these are drug/alcohol related.

White kids are more than twice as likely to die behind the wheel as Black kids.

The second leading cause of death among American teenagers is suicide. The teen suicide rate has tripled since 1960.

Over twice as many White kids will kill themselves as opposed to black kids. The suicide rate for White males 15-19 years in age is 2-1/2 times greater than that of Black males the same age.

Crime and Violence

According to the Annual Crime Reports published by the FBI, White Americans consistently commit the greatest share of virtually all crimes.

According to a CNN study, the typical perpetrator of campus crime is a 19 year old White male.

According to a New York Times study, Whites are the most likely racial group to engage in violence against all other groups -- Asian American, African American, Latinos, Gays, Lesbians, Jews, etc.

A May 1993 study by the Northeastern University Center for Applied Social Research concluded that 60% of those who commit urban hate crimes are White males.

According to the Wall Street Journal, Whites commit 54% of all violent crimes.

According to the Center for Disease Control, White teenagers have the fastest growing death rate from gunshot wounds, up 24% a year from 1988 through the early 1990's.

According to Gerry Spence, from his book "With Justice For None; Destroying An American Myth:"

a. The cost of corporate crime in America is over ten times greater than the combined larcenies, robberies, burglaries and auto thefts committed by individuals.

b. One in five of America's large corporations have been convicted of at least one major crime or has paid civil penalties for serious misbehavior.

c. According to a committee chaired by Senator Herb Kohl, Black youths are four times more likely to be incarcerated than Whites who commit the same crimes.

Welfare / Poverty / Illegitimacy

According to Ishmael Reed's book "AIRING DIRTY LAUNDRY,"

a. 2/3 of America's welfare recipients are White

b. 2/3 of America's welfare recipients live in rural areas

"Millions of White women are on welfare as a result of their husbands abandoning them."

"AIRING DIRTY LAUNDRY" by Ishmael Reed

* * * * *

"In relation to the entire U.S. population the proportion of White single mothers (37.9% in 1990) who live in poverty exceeds that for the entire Black population (29.3%)

According to the Children's Defense Fund, The fastest growing incidents of teenage pregnancies is occurring among White youths

2/3 Of the teens who gave birth each year are White.

2/3 Of the teens who give birth each year do not live in big cities.

50% Of the children who live in poverty, live in two parent homes in the suburbs and in rural areas.

Gangs

The Bloods and Crips are not the only gangs in America. According to the New York City Police, The most violent gang of the past twenty years was an Irish gang, The Westies. According to I.J. English in his book, "THE WESTIES," these were "the most brutal men this violent nation has ever seen. The Skinheads are a violent White gang as are many neo-Nazis. The Kehanihi is a terrorist Jewish gang in New York. Black gangs like the Bloods and Crips have no ability to engage in the international trade of guns and drugs that are transported by ship and airplanes.

Genetics / Crime

Many commentators are now claiming that Black crime is based on a Black tendency toward violence. This is absurd. Black People are of African descent. All of the ancient writers, from Homer of Greece to the Arab traveler Ibn Batutta, observed that Black Africans were the most peaceful, just and moral people in the world.

Genetics / Intelligence

Black People are not genetically inferior to Whites on the basis of intelligence. There are three simple arguments that can be put forward in support of this:

1. The first civilized people on earth were Black Africans. They were the original artists, architects, doctors, attorneys, scientists, priests, governors, etc.

   These Black achievements took place while White people lived in caves and were totally uncivilized. According to the ancient Greeks themselves, the ancient Blacks of Nubia and Egypt civilized them.

   During the Middle Ages, "Blackamoors" (i.e., Black Africans and mulatto Arabs) civilized southern Europe and this lead to the Age of Enlightenment and the Age of Discovery.

2. Before the busing plan was implemented in Los Angeles, a Black elementary school, Windsor Hills, had the highest reading test scores in the entire district. The reason for this is that Windsor Hills is an affluent Black community with a largely Black faculty at the school, which cared for and loved the children who attended each day.

3. A good example of what Black children can do when provided with full opportunities and a positive environment is happening in Great Britain today. According to a recent issue of The London Times:

   "Afro-Caribbean children in Great Britain have outscored native Whites for the first time since new testing procedures were established. The top score for an 8-year old was achieved by Jamaica born Natalie Windt who scored highest in English. She was further tested by researchers who noted that Blacks have, overall, scored higher than Whites in science and math too. The researchers observed that "strong parental support, high expectations, and unshakable motivation were the keys to this achievement."

BLACK PEOPLE PAID FOR AFFIRMATIVE ACTION WITH THEIR LIVES, AND ALL OF THE ATROCITIES THEY HAD TO ENDURE.

Look at the Faces of the Onlookers

THIS IS AMERICA
AMERICAN SLAVERY: HOW BAD WAS IT ?

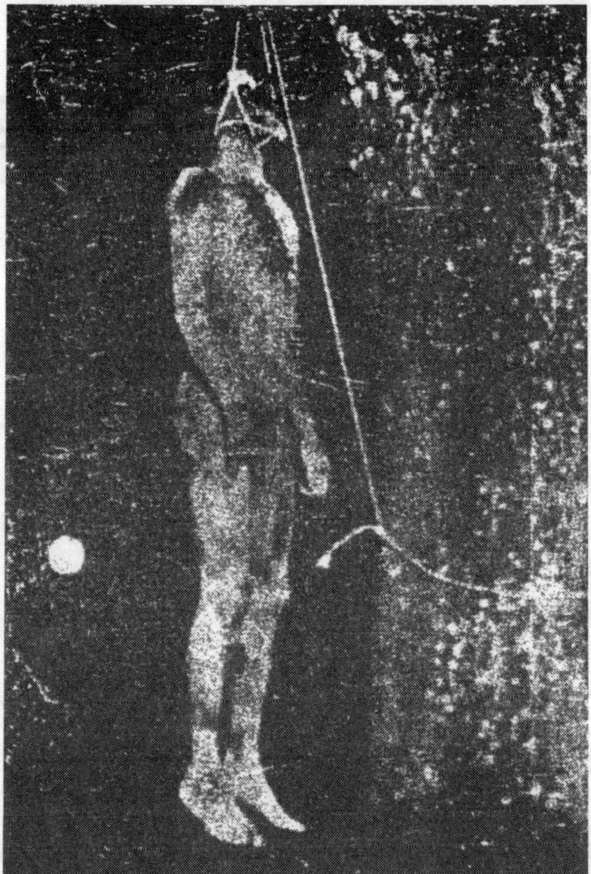

A victim of lynch-mob violence.
The fingers and penis have been
amputated by Klan members
for preserving in alcohol as
"souvenirs"

FISHER'S STUDIO DEMOREST, GA

This was a post card with the hanging on one side.

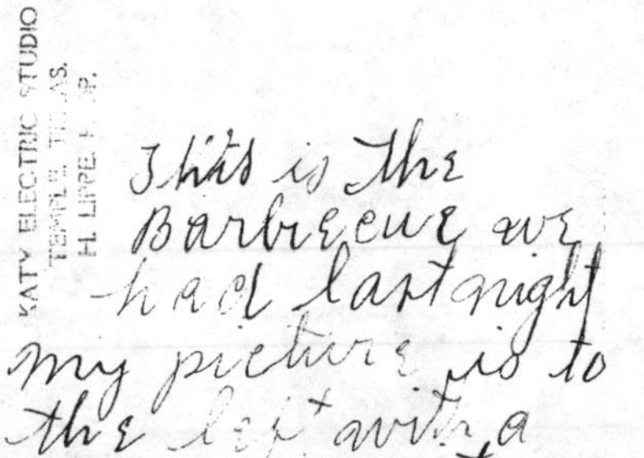
KATY ELECTRIC STUDIO

This is The Barbecue we had last night my picture is to the left with a cross over it your sone Joe.

The message says,
"This is the barbeque we had last night."

The Lynching of Laura Nelson.
May 25, 1911, Okemah, Oklahoma

THREE NEGROES
LYNCHED AT DULUTH,
MINN. FOR RAPE OCT. 1919
BY-M.P.S.

EVERY WEEKEND, all over the South and many Northern cities, PICK-A-NIGGER PARTIES were held. THEY WOULD LYNCH OR BURN A BLACK MAN TO A STAKE OR TIE THEM UP AND LIGHT A FIRE AROUND THEM. This happened all over, in towns, cities, and out in the country for over 300 years. These Black men were someone's husband, father, son, uncle, or close friend. If there were 50 killed per week for 300 years, that would have been 780,000 Black men slaughtered in American, only because they were black.

After the lynching and burning of Blacks, many of the people standing around would take fingers, ears, toes and sexual organs to save as souvenirs. Many of the pictures taken were made into post cards (such as the one on the following page) and mailed around.

* * * * *

Really, how bad was slavery? This is what happened to one family. However, these atrocities were repeated thousands of times.

From "WITHOUT SANCTUARY," p. 15:

> "A reporter for the Vicksburg Evening Post described the execution of the Holberts.
>
> "When the two Negroes were captured, they were tied to trees and while the funeral pyres were being prepared they were forced to suffer the most fiendish tortures. The blacks were forced to hold out their hands while one finger at a time was chopped off. The fingers were distributed as

souvenirs. The ears of the murderers were cut off. Holbert was beaten severely, his skull was fractured and one of his eyes, knocked out with a stick, hung by a shred from the socket. The most excruciating form of punishment consisted in the use of a large corkscrew in the hands of some of the mob. This instrument was bored into the flesh of the man and woman, in the arms, legs and body, and then pulled out, the spirals tearing out big pieces of raw, quivering flesh every time it was withdrawn."

**BLACK PEOPLE
PAID FOR AFFIRMATIVE ACTION
WITH THEIR LIVES,
AND ALL OF THE ATROCITIES
THEY HAD TO ENDURE.**

Chapter 4

BLACK HOLOCAUST
Over 100 Million Black People Slaughtered

Who Brought the Slaves to America ?

There were 128 registered slave ships. The first ship to bring captives was named "Good Ship Jesus." Its captain was John Hawkins. The owner of the ship was Queen Elizabeth I, ancestor of the present Queen Elizabeth of England.

The Library of Congress has the details on how many captives were on each ship. Some ships carried 10,442 captives, while others contained as many as 44,000. It is reported that over 100 million African captives perished during the Trans-Atlantic trip. Captives were packed on the ships like sardines. Those that were sick or were too weak for the trip were thrown overboard. Men, women and children were sacrificed into the murky waters.

Who brought the slaves to America is a question for the readers to research in order to get the answer. What were the names of the ships, the captains, and owners?

* * * * *

From The Jerusalem Chronicle, Vol. 5, No. 3, November /December 1994, Interview with Mr. Peoples.

In an interview with Mr. John Peoples (Peoples Helping People), he stated that he, "is dedicated to making sure

Blacks in this country know that over 100 million African slaves were kidnapped from the West Coast of Africa."

Mr. Peoples Helping People is the name of Mr. Peoples' organization. They chose April 19, 1995 as a day of remembrance for all the 100 million African slaves who perished during the Trans-Atlantic slave trade.

* * * * *

Reading from "AFRICA'S GIFT TO AMERICA"- p. 62
by J. A. Rogers

> "America's gain was Africa's great tragedy. The millions taken from her for 420 years (1440-1860), estimated by some at fifty million, set her back tremendously and that was not all; millions more were killed in slave raids.
>
> "A misconception was, that all captives came from Africa. Many captives came from the Blacks and Indians that already lived in America."

* * * * *

Reading from "100 YEARS OF LYNCHING" by Ralph Ginzburg

> "Between the years of 1859 to 1889 (30 years) over 5,000 Black People were lynched or burned to death."

Read the book for names of the victims.

* * * * *

Blacks paid for the right to receive preference. No other race, in the history of mankind, has had to withstand the atrocities, that the Black race has had to endure around the world and in the US; which includes: rape, lynching, burning at the stake, babies and children being used for alligator bait, dragging, being treated worse then animals, being called everything under the sun, etc. Some of these practices still go on today.

See section in this book entitled
"The Struggle Continues"

* * * * *

In June 2001, at a gathering for the National Commemoration of the Days of Remembrance, honoring the victims of the Jewish Holocaust, President George W. Bush told a group of cabinet members, congressional leaders and dignitaries from around the world, "There will come a time when the eye witnesses are gone; and that is why we are bound by conscience to remember what happened and to whom it happened."

Earlier, at the United States Holocaust Memorial Museum, President Bush stated, "We must never forget."

President Bush suffers from amnesia when it comes to remembering and recognizing the Black Holocaust.

* * * * *

Christopher Columbus Committe
Genocide on A Whole Race

When Christopher Columbus returned to America he went to Haiti with seventeen ships and more than 1,200 heavily armed men with horses and attack dogs. The original Haitians were called Arawaks or Tainos.

The source of information about what happened on the islands after Columbus arrived was noted by a Catholic priest named Bartolome De Las Casas, who lived in Haiti during the time of Columbus. Columbus' mission was to gather as much gold and as many slaves as possible. He went from island to island in the Caribbean taking Arawaks as captives. He ordered everyone over the age of 14, to produce specific quantities of gold every three months. If an Arawak could not produce this quota, Columbus then had his hands cut off, and left him to bleed to death. If the Arawaks tried to escape, they were hunted down by attack dogs and either hanged or burned alive.

The women were used as sex slaves and their children were murdered, then thrown into the sea. The Spaniards were so cruel, they thought nothing of cutting off slices of human flesh from Arawaks just to test the sharpness of their blades. Bishop De Las Casas wrote "My eyes have seen these acts; so foreign to human nature, that now I tremble as I write.

Within just two years three million Arawaks of Haiti died from murder, mutilation or suicide. Twenty- five years after Columbus entered Haiti; the Arawak population was reduced to zero; that is total annihilation or genocide.

The above is the Christopher Columbus that America celebrates with a holiday. Schools, cities, streets, etc. have been named after him when he was nothing but a butcher, a thief and a murderer.

For more detailed information, please read the truth about Christopher Columbus in the book, "BLACK PEOPLE & THEIR PLACE IN WORLD HISTORY."

Belgium King Leopold II
10 Million Black People Slaughtered

At the Berlin Conference (November 1884 to February 1885) where European countries met to decide how they would divide up Africa, King Leopold begged for the Congo Basin and guaranteed the well-being of the Congo's native population. He was given the Congo. Over a period of 25 years, Belgium King Leopold II was able to reduce the population of the Congo from 20 million to 10 million. His atrocities matched those of Christopher Columbus.

Both men proceeded to institute slavery among the native population and set quotas for individual production. Leopold chose to set quotas for ivory and rubber for each village. When a village fell short of it's quota, his solders brutally raided the village and cut off the right hands of the victims. Leopold's soldiers enjoyed summary executions followed by chopping of the victims' heads and placing them on poles around their gardens.

Please read the book "BLACK PEOPLE & THEIR PLACE IN WORLD HISTORY"

50 Thousand Haitians Slaughtered by U.S. Troops

In 1915, U.S. troops were sent to Haiti to put down a peasant rebellion. American Marines opened fire with machine guns from airplanes on defenseless Haitian villages, killing men, women, and children in the open market place.

From "ADDICTED TO WAR," #19, #20, by Joel Andreas

Slaughter of 1,200 Black Soldiers

In 1943, during World War II some 3,000 African American soldiers were sent to a U.S. Army base, Camp Van Dorn in Mississippi. They were members of the all Black 364th Infantry and were unwilling to endure the racial confines of the horribly segregated deep South.

It was clear that trouble would come. Within months, the townspeople were so upset that they threatened to take matters into their own hands to teach the, "niggers" their place. Of course, the "niggers" were not buying it. Things got so bad in the fall of 1943 that the Army ordered MP's, armed with 45 caliber machine guns and riding weapons carriers onto the base. At the same time it ordered the MP's to make sure that the Black soldiers had no firing pins in their guns. At night the MP's pulled up to the Black camp and ordered the Black soldiers into an area. The MP's opened fire on everything that moved, shot into the barracks, and shot them out of trees, where some were trying to hide. They shot every "nigger" they could find.

When the shooting stopped, over 1,200 members of the 364th were slaughtered. Their bodies were loaded on boxcars and stacked inside like pulpwood. They were buried in long trenches dug by bulldozers. This is a true story, told by one of the MP's following orders.

Received from the Internet
No Copyright or Author Noted
Posted in the Interest of Black People's Education

The story was turned into a book. Please read:
"THE SLAUGHTER - AN AMERICAN ATROCITY"
by Carroll Case.

Go to the web site:
www.theslaughter.com/frontcvr.html

Bombs Dropped on American Blacks in 1921

Approximately 3,000 Black men, women and children were slaughtered and over 600 successful businesses were destroyed in Tulsa, Oklahoma in 1921. They included, 21 churches, 21 restaurants, 30 grocery stores, two movie theaters, a hospital, a bank, a post office, libraries, schools, law offices, a half dozen private Airplanes and a bus system

All of the above happen because a nineteen year-old Black man named Dick Rowland accidentally stepped on the foot of the elevator operator, Sarah Page, a White woman.

Taken from
"BLACK PEOPLE & THEIR PLACE IN HISTORY

Also, read the book
"BLACK WALL STREET: A LOST DREAM"
by Ron Wallace and Jay Wilson

Go to:

www. Afro-American Almanac.com
HYPERLINK http://
www.toptags.com/aama/events/oklahoma.htm
www.toptags.com/aama/events/oklahoma.htm
www.toptags.com/aama/events/okriot.htm

* * * * *

From "THE TADDLER," May, 1994, Vol. 1, No. 3
(A NEWSLETTER FOR THINKERS)

> "After the bombing in Tulsa, more than 4,000 Blacks were confined in animal shelters and not allowed in public without a green pass. No Whites were interned. During the cold winter 1,000 Blacks were forced to live in tents."

Houston Riots and Court Martial of 1917

On August 23, 1917, a Houston police officer patrolling the San Felipe district (Black business district), badly beat two Black soldiers in separate incidents. In the second instance, the victim was a provost guard (MP) who was attempting to question the officer about the earlier assault.

The soldiers were members of the Black Twenty-Fourth Infantry Regiment that was stationed in Houston, Texas. Having had previous problems with the townspeople and police, the soldiers felt that their superior officers would do nothing about the incident. About 100 Black soldiers picked up their Springfield rifles and marched to Houston.

When they arrived in the San Felipe district they fought a running battle with members of the Houston police, elements of other White military units stationed in the city and some of the communities leading citizens.

The men of the Twenty-Fourth were Black; their opponents White. Before the confrontation ended, 20 persons were dead or mortally wounded in the only racially motivated riot in United States history to claim more White lives than Black. Four Blacks died.

Court-martials hung 19 soldiers from the Twenty-Fourth Infantry Regiment without appeals or review of the case by the President or the Secretary of War.

For the complete story read: "THE HOUSTON RIOT AND COURT MARTIAL OF 1917"
Produced by: Carver Community Cultural Center
San Antonio, Texas

East St. Louis Riot of 1917

In East St. Louis, Illinois a White mob of over 3,000 on May 28, 1917, ravaged African American stores, homes and churches. Over 100 Blacks were gunned down as they left their burning homes, including a small child who was shot and thrown back into the burning building to die.

Riots at Rosewood, Florida

Rosewood was a Black town founded after 1870. It was developed and run by Black People.

A White woman (who had an adulterous lifestyle) in another town not far from Rosewood, falsely accused a Black stranger of raping her. A White mob of over 1,000 burned down Rosewood and murdered all the Black People that did not escape. No true figures are available on how many were slaughtered. This was considered one of the worst race riots in America. Look at the movie "Rosewood."

Rebellion - 1992 In Los Angeles

The same conditions exist today that existed for poor people (Blacks, Mexicans, Asians etc), during the Los Angeles Rebellion in 1965. Recommendations made by the Warren Commission were not implemented. However, a review of news videos and private. Videos of the rebellion in 1992 show that Blacks (outside the Black community) were not the largest group of looters, yet they got most of the blame. In Korean town, Blacks were blamed for most of the looting, however, they were the minority living in the area. After the riots there were many meetings among numerous religious groups to start a healing process among the races. News coverage showed some of the meetings and what was suppose to be a "Healing Process." The following letter was distributed throughout the community.

Message to Those At the Healing Tables
"It's Time To Heal"

It's time to heal they say, so they joined hands bowed their heads, prayed for peace and the healing process to began. Many of those bowed heads praying for healing, are only seeking to return to the same mentality and actions that existed prior to the riot. They are not aware, that until the world accept the truth; face the reality of history by teaching the contributions to the development of this country by Afro-Americans, there will be no true healing. Until the world changes its perception of Black People there will be no peace. Young Afro-Americans are tired of the same old lies.

For the past few days I have watched the innocent look of Orientals on television asking "WHY?" They forgot the manner in which they treat Afro-Americans, prior to the riot. I can remember when many of the large indoor swap meets owned or controlled by Orientals opened in the Black neighborhoods. When an Afro-American business person attempted to rent a space in the swap meet, they were either flatly refused or told only members of the Oriental corporation were allowed to rent in their locations.

Sometimes after community pressure, the Orientals would rent to one or two Afro-American businesspersons. One or two out of 50 or 100? This will no longer be accepted. Will the healing change this practice? Why, they cried? I remember when I have gone into several, inside swap meets, controlled by Orientals. From the time I stepped in the door, I was followed and made to feel uneasy; as if I were going to steal something. A Korean lady, interviewed on television after the riot stated, "They all steal." Many of the Oriental merchants don't understand what some of their problems are in the Afro-

American communities. Perhaps I can share a few thoughts with them.

First, many Koreans think Afro-Americans are illiterate and Koreans are more intelligent. I'm speaking of several experiences I have had and many of my friends have shared the same situations. Many Orientals think Black People can't count. Today at a city council meeting, Orientals were saying their "little businesses didn't make much money." We can count, and when you over charge it adds up to a good profit. Add years to this practice and a lot of money has been made. Stop fooling yourselves.

Second, when people are continually verbally abused, insulted, taken advantage of by overcharging (when they know they are being overcharged) and just not given respect; they react in different ways. This is legal stealing from those that they take advantage of. Some people who feel they have been taken advantage of may steal. Others may hold their frustration until they feel the time is right. Then they loot and burn. Will healing cause the Oriental business people to change their attitudes? I remember when a friend of mine attempted to return some defective merchandise but was unable to because of the NO REFUND POLICY, UNDER ANY CIRCUMSTANCES.

When will the healing start?

There was a Korean woman on television crying and saying, "We work hard, we do not have much money, our clothes are not too expensive." I don't know where her store was located, however, most Korean businesses in the Black community sell their products at a much higher cost, yielding a large profit margin. Face the truth, it might prevent the next burning.

Most Orientals selling at swap meets import most of their merchandise, paying little of nothing for it, then adding a large markup. Most of the merchandise is inferior and cheaply made. After a few weeks, a lot of it comes apart. Most of the customers of the swap meets live in low-income areas and are trying to stretch their dollars. They are looking for deals. Most of the time, all they get is junk. Could you say these stores are taking advantage of these low-income families? The owners know most of their merchandise is inferior. That's why the no return policy.

What does the healing process mean? What will it produce? If the healing process will only return us to the same mental attitudes and actions, I don't think it will work. It's time to face the facts that created the problems in the first place.

Received as a Handout
Source Unknown and Author Unknown
Posted in the Interest of Black People's Education

FROM BIRTH
"NO ONE IS BORN
A THUG OR CRIMINAL,
BUT CONDITIONS OF LIFE
BREED THEM."
By: Dr. Romeo L. Taylor, Sr.

There are many more atrocities against Black People such as the "Red Summer" and the "Riots at Elaine, Arkansas." Over a period of 400 years, there were many more slaughters and atrocities that have not been revealed yet. City officials and sheriffs were a part of the Ku Klux Klan, so they were able to keep it quiet. Remember the unnamed thousands that were terrorized and murdered at the "pick-a-nigger" parties. Can you imagine every weekend all over the South, someone's father, son, brother or uncle was selected and murdered only because he was Black. Sometimes their crime was only "looking in the direction of a White woman."

Branding Slaves,
On the Coast of Africa Previous to Embarkation

Chapter 5

REPARATIONS

What does Reparations for African Americans really mean? According to The Southern California Reparation United Front, "Reparations means getting the American government, which supported the institution of slavery, lynching, institutional racism and other such things, to admit that it did a great injury to Black People in this country, that the injury still continues, that the government apologizes by compensating Black People.

There are people opposed to Reparation payments stating, "Slavery was legal." How can a person justify lynching, burning people alive, raping women, girls and boys, only because they were Black. What laws are they referring to? Man's law or God's Law? Anyone whose mindset believes those actions were justified because it was legal, is sick.

The forms that Reparations will take will be decided by Black People talking together about that issue. It may be a 50-year trust fund accessible to any Black person who wants to start a business. It may be a guaranteed scholarship to and through college for every Black American high school graduate. It may be any of those and any of various other forms that we can generally agree on. Some money will probably be involved but that will be only a small part of a much larger equation. Reparations will come from the American government, not individual White people."

We feel the name African American, as a racial identity, should be changed to Black African Americans. White people born in Africa and their children that move to America are also African Americans. We don't feel our oppressors in Africa, nor their descendants, are entitled to be paid for the suffering they caused on Black People. However, if we push for Reparations only under the name of African Americans, "White African Americans" would be entitled to the same benefits as Blacks.

* * * * *

A BILL IS COMING FOR

400 YEARS OF

FORCED, SLAVE LABOR

Reported History of Reparations Payments

"What Is The Matter With This Picture ?"

1990	USA	$1.6 Billion or $20,000 Each	Japanese American
1990	Austria	$25 Million to Holocaust Survivors	Jewish Claims Of Austria
1988	Canada	250,000 Square Miles of Land	Indians and Eskimos
1988	Canada	$230 Million	Japanese Canadians
1986	USA	$32 Million 1839 Treaty	Ottawas of Michigan
1985	USA	$31 Million	Chippewas of Michigan
1985	USA	$12.3 Million	Seminoles of Florida
1985	USA	$105 Million	Sioux of South Dakota
1980	USA	$81 Million	Klamaths of Oregon
1971	USA	$1 Billion+44Billion Acres of Land	Alaska Natives Land Settlement
1952	Germany	$822 Million to Holocaust Survivors	German Jewish Settlement
1865 -2003	USA	$0	Africans

Courtesy of Mr. Peoples Helping People

MILLIONS MURDERED THEN & MILLIONS STARVING NOW
Stolen from Africa
ONE HUNDRED MILLION PEOPLE
AND
TRILLIONS IN:
GOLD
OIL
COPPER
TIN
SILVER
NATURAL GAS
TEA
GUM
PERFUME OILS
BANANAS
BAUXITE
LAND
TIMBER
CHROME
KOLA NUTS
SOLDIERS
DIAMONDS
PINEAPPLES
POTASSIUM
PLATINUM
LEATHER
CATTLE
COTTON
ALUMINUM
URANIUM
COFFEE
IVORY
RUBBER
PHOSPHATES
PALM OIL
LEAD
SUGAR
ANIMALS
FISH
ARTIFACTS
MANGANESE
COCOA
IRON
LABOR
PEANUTS
COBALT
ZINC
POLITICAL,
ECONOMIC
POWER
TOBACCO
LIMESTONE
& MUCH, MUCH MO

IT'S BLACK REPARATIONS TIME

REPATRIATIONS - RETRIBUTIONS & COMPOUNDED INTERESTS AND PENALTIES NOW PAST DUE AND DEMANDED FROM:

PORTUGAL; ENGLAND; AMERICA (NORTH & SOUTH); BELGIUM; FRANCE; GERMANY; THE DUTCH; SPAIN; ITALY; ISRAEL; JAPAN; ARABIA; SOVIET UNION; SOUTH AFRIKAANS WORLD-TRADERS-RULERS; INDIAN MIDDLEMEN; LEBANESE MIDDLEMEN; SOUTH AFRICA AND ALL COUNTRIES, BUSINESSES AND INDIVIDUALS DOING OR WHO HAVE DONE BUSINESS WITH SOUTH AFRICA SUCH AS U.S.A, CANADA, JAPAN, ISRAEL, EUROPE, SOUTH AMERICA, SOVIET UNION, IBM AND OTHERS; CECIL RHODES SCHOLARSHIP FUND; BARCLAY'S BANK; LLOYDS BANK; FIRESTONE RUBBER; SHELL OIL; MOBIL OIL; LEVER BROS.; DE BEERS DIAMONDS & GOLD MINES; GENERAL MOTORS; FORD MOTORS; ROTHSCHILDS; J.P. MORGAN; OXFORD UNIVERSITY; WESTMINSTER BANK; STANDARD BANK; NATIONAL PROVINCIAL BANK; PROCTOR & GAMBLE; GULF OIL; CADBURY & FRY; LIPTON TEA; RAND CORPORATION; NATIONAL BANK OF BELGIUM; FARRELL SHIPPING LINES; UNITED FRUIT CO.; UNITED STATES STEEL; BRITISH MUSEUM OF STOLEN ART; MUSEUMS OF PARIS, BERLIN, NEW YORK; WORLD BANK; TRI-LATERAL COMMISSION, INTERNATIONAL MONETARY FUND; ARAB REPUBLICS OF NORTHERN AFRICA AND MANY, MANY OTHERS.

YOUR PAYBACK TO AFRICA* INCLUDES MONEY - TECHNOLOGY - SCIENCE - TRADE

"ALL THE WEALTH THE WHITE MAN HAS TODAY (1919) WILL NOT BE ENOUGH TO PAY THE BLACKS WHEN THE BLACKS PRESENT THEIR BILL." - MARCUS GARVEY

"IF YOU ARE THE SON OF A MAN WHO HAD A WEALTHY ESTATE AND YOU INHERITED YOUR FATHER'S ESTATE YOU HAVE TO PAY THE DEBTS THAT YOUR FATHER INCURRED. THE ONLY REASON THE PRESENT GENERATION OF WHITE AMERICANS ARE IN THE POSITION OF ECONOMIC STRENGTH IS THEIR FATHERS WORKED OUR FATHERS/MOTHERS FOR OVER 400 YEARS WITH NO PAY." - MALCOM X

DEMAND ALL WESTERN GOVERNMENTS, CORPORATIONS, NORTH AFRICAN AND MIDDLE EASTERN ARABS AND ISRAEL IMMEDIATELY AID AFRICA'S STARVING MILLIONS WITH SELF-HELP TYPE ASSISTANCE. ALSO, TO STOP ALL ACTIVITY WHICH PROMOTES APARTHIED AND SELF-DESTRUCTIVE POLITICAL VIOLENCE AND COUPS IN AFRICA.

WRITE CONGRESS TODAY - SUPPORT THE AFRICAN-AMERICAN REPARATION BILL H.R. 3745 BY CONGRESSMAN JOHN CONYERS.

AS FOR YOU PERSONALLY, DO MORE TO HELP AFRICA RIGHT NOW!

*IT IS AFRICA THAT SUFFERED THE LOSS. THAT'S WHY WE BLACKS ARE IN THE WESTERN WORLD AND THE WESTERN WORLD IS SO WEALTHY.

BY GUBOA WA ARATHI

REVISED 1991

The United States also contributed, after the wars, to rebuild Japan, Germany, Vietnam, and Korea. Now Congress has allocated billions of dollars for its war on terrorism.

The U.S. Congress reportedly paid Japanese Americans $1.6 billion for taking their property and holding them in camps for four years during World War II. Yet they are not willing to pay Blacks for being held for over 400 years as free labor. Black People's free labor resulted in millions of jobs and trillions of dollars in income for the United States. Blacks picked cotton that was exported all over the world.

Common sense tells you there is something wrong with this practice, yet the silent majority won't speak up. Some say, "Racism does not exist to day." We say, "Put your money, where your mouth is." The proof of the pudding is in the eating.

* * * * *

The Struggle Continues

There are some Blacks and many Whites that live in denial about continued discrimination in the world today. The biggest supporter of discrimination is the "Silent Majority," those people that still go along with acts of racism without speaking up. Below are a few examples of discrimination and hate crimes.

Jet Magazine
July 19, 1999
Amtrak Pay $8 Million
To Settle Racial
Discrimination Lawsuit

Jet Magazine
November 29, 1999
NY City Cracks Down On
Cabdrivers Who Won't
Stop For Blacks

Jet Magazine
April 10, 2000
Adam's Mark Hotel Chain Pay
$8 Million To Settle Discrimination Lawsuits

San Fernando Valley News
March 1999
Two Nazi Low Riders Charged with Attempted
Murder and Assault with A Deadly Weapon
Upon a Black Man

Jet Magazine
January 10, 2000
Black Man Jailed
19 Years for Rape of
White Woman Found
Innocent and Released
and Released

Jet Magazine
October 2, 2000
Study Shows
Justice Dept. Lawyers
Seek Death Penalty
Most for Minorities

Los Angeles Sentinel
July 5, 2001
Black-Owned Oil Company
Suing Exxon for $10 Billion

Jet Magazine
July 19, 1999
Suit Filed Accusing
Microsoft of Linking
Blacks to Monkeys
On Computer Program

Jet Magazine
January 24, 2000
Black Colleges Across
U.S. Targets of Hate Mail

News from the Radio
September 25, 1998
Black Texas Man, James Byrd, Jr.,
Was Assaulted by Three White Men,
Chained to the Back of a Truck and
Dragged Alive to his Death

News from the Radio
May 17, 1998
Back to the Past
At Taylor County High School in Butler, Georgia,
White Students Voted to Have a
Segregated Prom for 2003.
No Black Students Were Invited
This Was a Return to the
31-Year Tradition of Separate Proms
Last year's prom was integrated.

The headlines and news items above are only examples to show the struggle continues. Every year, hundreds of claims are filed and won.

* * * * *

BLACK PEOPLE ARE
LIKE TIMEX WATCHES
"WE TAKE A LICKIN,
BUT WE KEEP ON TICKING!"

Chapter 6

PAST BLACK PRESIDENTS OF THE UNITED STATES

Is this John Hanson ?

Taken from
www.dickgregory.com

John Hanson - First President of thc United States November 5, 1781 to November 3, 1782

A lot of the information we expose in this book has been covered up, altered or the people in power have attempted to eliminate from history.

During the time of slavery, in the North, there were powerful Black land owners who had slaves, both White and Black.

At the signing of the Declaration of Independence, there was a Black man sitting in the first seat on the left side of the table. He has never been identified by name in any history book. See copy of a $2.00 bill below.

Note the First Man Sitting at the
Left Side of the Table

John Hanson was the most powerful and clever politician at that time. Therefore, it is easy to believe that man was John Hanson, the Moor, who later became the first President of the United States. John Hanson is called "the forgotten man."

John Hanson was elected to the Provincial Legislature of Maryland in 1775 and became a member of Congress in 1777.

The Articles of Confederation was proposed on June 11, 1776. At this point, the 13 original colonies were not a national government. Maryland would not sign the Articles unless Virginia and New York signed first. Maryland was afraid these states would gain too much power in the new government, having such large areas of land.

The Articles of Confederation were agreed to by Congress on November 15, 1777 and became law after ratification by Maryland on March 1, 1781.

After the Revolutionary War ended, a president was needed to run the new country. John Hanson was unanimously chosen by Congress (which included George Washington) as the first president.

Immediately the troops demanded to be paid. They threatened to overthrow the new government and put Washington on the throne as King. All the members of Congress ran for their lives, leaving Hanson as the only person left running the government.

Hanson was able to calm the troops by sending 800 pounds of sterling silver to George Washington to provide the troops with shoes.

As President, Hanson ordered all foreign troops off American soil and removed all foreign flags. Also, as President of the United States, Hanson established the Great Seal of the United States that all presidents have since been required to use on all official documents.

Hanson also declared that the fourth Thursday of every November was to be Thanks Giving Day; which is still true today.

A president under the Confederation could only serve for one year. Those following John Hanson was: Elias Boudinot (1783); Thomas Miffin (1784); Richard Henry Lee (1785); Nathan Gorman (1786); Arthur St. Clair (1787) and Cyrus Griffin (1788), all prior to Washington taking office.

13 Original Colonies

The thirteen original states that formed the Confederation were: New Hampshire, Massachusetts, Rhode Island, Connecticut, New York, New Jersey, Pennsylvania, Delaware, Maryland, Virginia, North Carolina, South Carolina and Georgia. However, there was a problem with the government under the Articles of Confederation. The individual states had too much power and nothing could be agreed upon. Therefore, a new doctrine needed to be written.

Thus, the Constitution of the United States was adopted, with George Washington becoming the first president under the constitution, but George Washington was not the first President of the United States; he was the 8th.

John Hanson, was the heir of one of the greatest family traditions in the colonies and became the patriarch of a long line of American patriots - his great-grandfather died at the Lutzen beside the great King Aldophus Gustavus of Sweden. See the story of King Aldophus Gustavus under The Past Black Kings and Royalty of Sweden.

For more information go to:
www.dickgregory.com/dick/14_washington.html

We've been told that an etching of the signing of the Declaration of Independence hangs on the wall of the Capitol Rotunda. There is a Black man sitting at the table; we believe that man was John Hanson.

Five Negro Presidents of the United States ....
"According to What White People Say"

Note: J.A. Rogers named four Negro Presidents, the fifth Negro President's name had not been confirmed. However, the book, "THE SIX BLACK PRESIDENTS: BLACK BLOOK, WHITE MASKS - USA," identifies the president not named in "FIVE NEGRO PRESIDENTS," plus it lists Lincoln's Black Vice-President, to make a count of six.

The book "BLACK PEOPLE & THEIR PLACE IN WORLD HISTORY" identifies Calvin Coolidge as having strong Black blood. We are sure as time goes on, others will be discovered.

One must understand the conditions of Blacks in this country caused many Blacks that could pass for White, to do so. Those that passed for White, in order to conceal their past would often overly display dislikes for Blacks.

For a more in-depth study of their mindset, Please read
"THE SIX BLACK PRESIDENTS:
BLACK BLOOD, WHITE MASKS - USA"

Warren G. Harding - 29th President (1921–1923)

The writer Irving Wallace wrote a book entitled "THE MAN." It was the story of a Black Vice President of the United States, who became President. Many Black historians believed the character was Warren G. Harding.

President Harding
and
His Paternal Grand Uncle, Oliver Harding.

Before the 1920 elections, Democratic papers stated Harding "was a Negro." Millions of mimeographed broadsides had been distributed stating "Harding's father is George Tyron Harding, obviously a mulatto; he has thick lips, rolling eyes, and chocolate skin, and his mother Phoebe Dickerson, a midwife, "little is known about her ancestry; she was White.

The Attorney General at that time was Harry Daugherty. He said that there was discovered in the San Francisco mails alone, over 250,00 copies and "President Wilson indignantly ordered them destroyed." Thereafter they were distributed by hand.

See additional information in

"THE FIVE NEGRO PRESIDENTS" by J.A. Rogers
"SEX AND RACE, VOL. II" p. 248

Also read: "THE SIX BLACK PRESIDENTS: BLACK BLOOD, WHITE MASKS - USA"

Thomas Jefferson - 3rd President (1800-1808)

The chief attack on Jefferson was in "The Johnny Cake Papers." In a general denunciation of him it said, "Tom Jefferson, son of a half breed Indian squaw, sired by a Virginian mulatto father." It also called him a "Half-Nigger."

See additional information in

"THE FIVE NEGRO PRESIDENTS" by J.A. Rogers

Andrew Jackson - 7th President (1828-1836)

Andrew Jackson's father and mother came from Ireland and were wretchedly poor. The Virginia Magazine of History, Vol. 29, p. 191, says that Jackson was the son of a White woman who had "intermarried with a Negro and his eldest brother had been sold as a slave in Carolina." What gave an air of truth to this was the elder Jackson died before Andrew was born. His widow went to live on the Crawford farm where there were Negro slaves and one of these was Andrew's father. It was stressed that Andrew was conceived after the death of his supposed father, whose name he bore.

See additional information in

"THE FIVE NEGRO PRESIDENTS" by J.A. Rogers

Abraham Lincoln - 16th President (1860-1865)

Lincoln was said to be the illegitimate son of a Negro by Nancy Hanks. In his campaign for the Presidency he was often referred to as a Negro by his opponents and was called "Abraham Africanas the First."

Lincoln said of his father, "His face was round, his complexion swarthy, hair black and coarse, eyes brown." Of himself, of dark complexion with coarse black hair and dark eyes. Herndon, his closest friend and a law partner said he had "very dark skin." Herndon said, "There was something about Lincoln's origin he never cared to dwell on."

Herndon says, "Lincoln often thought of committing suicide. Why? Did the knowledge of his mother's origin or his own press the thought of suicide upon him?" (THE HIDDEN LINCOLN, p. 412,1938).

Jacobson mentions a "Catechism" by a "Western author producing evidence' that Lincoln was of Negro ancestry. Read Coleman, Wm. "THE EVIDENCE THAT ABRAHAM LINCOLN WAS NOT BORN IN LAWFUL WEDLOCK," 1899. Abe Lincoln was called Abraham Africanas the First, baboon, monster, idiot, mulatto, etc. He was threatened with flogging, hanging, burning at the stake and death.

Abraham Lincoln - Cartoon of 1860
Note Lincoln's wooly hair.

Many more books of reference are listed concerning Abraham Lincoln's birth in "THE FIVE NEGRO PRESIDENTS," "THE SIX BLACK PRESIDENTS: BLACK BLOOK, WHITE MASKS - USA," and "THE HIDDEN LINCOLN," p. 411.

There is a misconception of the Emancipation Proclamation by most people. The President threatened the rebelling Southern states that, if they did not end their fighting and rejoin the Union by January 1, 1863, he would set all slaves free in those rebellious states.

Lincoln's Emancipation Proclamation permitted the retention of the slaves in those slave states, which were fighting for the Union, as well as in those parishes and counties in sympathy with him. He also excluded Tennessee, hoping that it would join the Union. In the words of the Proclamation those states were to continue holding their slaves "precisely as if this proclamation were not issued." Slavery was not abolished by the Emancipation Proclamation but by the Thirteenth Amendment of the Constitution.

Had the South stopped fighting and rejoined the Union, no slaves would have been set free. President Lincoln issued his Preliminary Emancipation on September 22, 1862.

* * * * *

Preliminary Emancipation Proclamation, 1862

> "On the first day of January... all persons held as slaves within any State, or designated part of a State, the people whereof shall then be in rebellion against the United States shall be then, hence forward and forever free."

President Abraham Lincoln
Preliminary Emancipation Proclamation
September 22, 1862

(See complete Emancipation Proclamation in United States Documents section of this book)

* * * * *

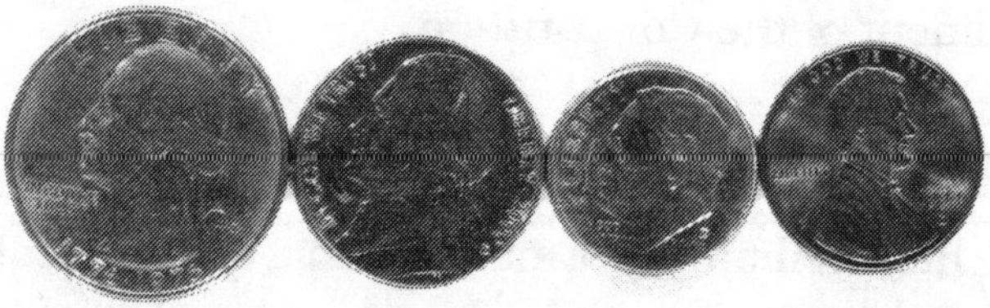

Why was the coin of Lincoln made out of copper, when constitutionally only silver or gold could be used as legal tender? Copper is brown. Why was the face of Lincoln faced in another direction from the rest of the presidents? Was there a statement in doing so?

Many more books of reference are listed concerning Abraham Lincoln's birth in "THE FIVE NEGRO PRESIDENTS," "THE SIX BLACK PRESIDENTS; BLACK BLOOD, WHITE MASKS - USA," "100 AMAZING FACTS ABOUT THE NEGRO" (with complete proof) and "THE HIDDEN LINCOLN," p. 411.

As we mentioned before many Black People that passed for White, had to openly show a dislike for Blacks thereby misleading the White public. Lerone Bennett, social historian and author of many books, including "BEFORE THE MAYFLOWER," stated in the February 8, 1968 issue of Jet Magazine, "Lincoln made his position crystal clear. He was opposed, Lincoln said, to Negro citizenship and to the niggers and White people marrying together." In addition, Lincoln opposed the Underground Railroad, which aided runaway slaves and publicly announced his support of the fugitive slave law.

Hannibal Hamlin - Lincoln's Vice President (1860 - 1864)

Southern papers brought out a story that Hannibal Hamlin, of Maine, was part Negro. Hannibal Hamlin only served as Vice President for one term. Andrew Johnson became Lincoln's Vice President in his second term and assumed the presidency from 1865-1868, following Lincoln's assassination.

* * * * *

Dwight D. Eisenhower - 34th President (1952 - 1960)

They say a picture is worth a thousand words.

President Dwight D Eisenhower's
Father and Mother

Read the story in:

"THE SIX BLACK PRESIDENTS:
BLACK BLOOD, WHITE MASKS - USA"

Calvin Coolidge - 30th President (1923 - 1928)

Calvin Coolidge proudly admitted that his mother was dark because of mixed Indian ancestry. However, Dr. BaKhufu says, "By 1800, the New England Indian was hardly any longer pure Indian, because they had mixed so often with Blacks." Calvin Coolidge's Mother's maiden name was "Moor". In Europe the name "Moor" was given to all Black People, just as the name Negro was used in America.

As time goes on, we may find there are other United States Presidents that have Black blood.

For more information read:

"THE SIX BLACK PRESIDENTS:
BLACK BLOOD, WHITE MASKS - USA"
THE FIVE NEGRO PRESIDENTS
BLACK PEOPLE & THEIR PLACE IN WORLD HISTORY

* * * * *

A Surprise on the $10 Bill

Black Alexander Hamilton

The ancestry of Alexander Hamilton was long disputed. However, native Virgin Islanders had insisted he was colored, while White American authors deny it.

The surest proof that Hamilton was of Negro ancestry says Rev. Martin, was Hamilton's brother, James, same mother, same father, migrated to the United States where he was treated as a Negro because of his color and hair. James "was once refused a seat in a Broadway

Alexander Hamilton - Drawn from life by Peale
Hamilton was darker in color than the picture shows. Note his wool-ish hair.

Alexander Hamilton - Caucasionized

coach because of his dark complexion and sued the company for heavy damages," quotes Rev. Martin from a letter to the Times.

The Spokesman Magazine, January 1925, insisted that Hamilton's "Negro extraction has never been successfully disputed. The statesman had Negro blood, his mother being a Negro woman."

The real truth of Hamilton's ancestry can be found in the earliest and least known portrait of him. In this he is seen with that kind of wool-ish hair common among light Negroes in the West Indies. There is also a certain fullness about the mouth that is somewhat Negroid. The portrait is by Peale.

For additional information read:

"THE FIVE NEGRO PRESIDENTS"

"THE SIX BLACK PRESIDENTS:
BLACK BLOOD, WHITE MASKS - USA"

* * * * *

Chapter 7

BLACK RECONSTRUCTION

When the Civil War ended, there were 5 million Whites and 4 million blacks in the south. Out of these numbers, 700,00 Blacks and 660,00 Whites were registered to vote at the beginning of Reconstruction.

Almost 200,000 Whites could not register to vote or hold public office because of their participation in the rebellion. These were large figures, considering the fact that 18-year olds and women could not vote.

As a result of the politician organization of the new freemen, Blacks had statewide voting majority in Louisiana, Alabama, Mississippi, Florida and South Carolina. In South Carolina, there were 84 Blacks in the first Reconstruction Legislature. Blanche K. Bruce was one of two Blacks who served as U.S. Senators from Mississippi, considered by many to be the most liberal state in the union. William H. Lewis was Assistant Attorney General of the United States from 1911-1913.

P.B.S. Pinchback became Governor of Louisiana, Robert Wood was Mayor of Natchez, Mississippi, and W. Cunez ran for Mayor of Galveston, Texas. Under Black representative leadership, the South was rising again.

The Black Reconstruction only lasted for a brief ten years. Black elected officials were driven from office or assassinated. By 1880, 130,000 Blacks and White Republicans who voted against legal re-enslavement, union men and loyal southern Whites were murdered by terrorist organizations (Southern Democrats, Ku Klux

Klan and White supremacists). Former slaveholders and White supremacists believed Blacks had been created solely for the use of Whites. They wanted slavery back, along with its free Black labor.

For additional information on Blacks during the Reconstruction Period read:

"VALLEY OF THE DRY BONES"
"THE LONGEST STRUGGLE" in Tony Brown's Journal
First Quarter 1985, Page 10

* * * * *

"Sparkling Gems"

The book, "Sparkling Gems," published in 1897, tells the story about the progress of the Negro after slavery, during segregation.

Blacks owned a total of over $400,000,000, free from all encumbrances. This was during a time when the dollar had value. When segregation existed, Black People only spent money with each other. Therefore, the Black Dollar circulated within the Black community.

Black Wall Street in Oklahoma was an example. There were over 600 successful businesses, which included 21 churches, 21 restaurants, 30 grocery stores, 2 movie theaters, a hospital, a bank, a post office, libraries, schools, law offices, a half dozen private airplanes and a bus system.

All over the nation, Black businesses were thriving with a lot of Black business people getting rich. Every Black person that wanted a job had one.

SPARKLING GEMS

OF

RACE KNOWLEDGE WORTH READING.

A COMPENDIUM OF VALUABLE INFORMATION AND WISE SUGGESTIONS THAT WILL INSPIRE NOBLE EFFORT AT THE HANDS OF EVERY RACE-LOVING MAN, WOMAN, AND CHILD.

ILLUSTRATED WITH SUPERB HALF-TONE ENGRAVINGS.

COMPILED AND ARRANGED BY
JAMES T. HALEY.

SOLD BY SUBSCRIPTION,
PRICE, $1.25.

"*Give attendance to reading.*" (*1 Tim. iv. 13.*)
"*No man has a right to bring up his children without surrounding them with good books. A book is better than sleep for weariness.*" (*Henry Ward Beecher.*)

NASHVILLE, TENN.:
J. T. HALEY & COMPANY, PUBLISHERS.
1897.

Published in 1897

CONTENTS.

(7)

From "Sparkling Gems"

"Sparkling Gems," published in 1897, lists the following statistics as to the diversified wealth of the New Negro in the Union, this was given out as official in:

Alabama	$10,120,137	New Jersey	$3,637,832
Arkansas	$9,810,346	North Carolina	$13,481,717
California	$4,416,939	New Mexico	$395,244
Colorado	$3,400,527	North Dakota	$84,101
Connecticut	$550,170	Ohio	$8,580,000
Delaware	$1,320,196	Oklahoma	$4,213,408
Florida	$8,690,044	Oregon	$93,500
Georgia	$15,196,885	Pennsylvania	$16,730,639
Idaho	$16,411	Rhode Island	$3,740,000
Illinois	$11,889,562	South Carolina	$16,750,121
Indiana	$4,404,524	Utah	$82,500
Massachusetts	$9,904,524	South Dakota	$136,787
Michigan	$5,200,122	Tennessee	$11,446,292
Minnesota	$1,210,259	Texas	$32,852,995
Mississippi	$16,742,349	Vermont	$1,112,731
Missouri	$8,366,474	Virginia	$10,932,009
Montana	$132,419	Washington	$632,515
Nebraska	$2,750,000	West Virginia	$6,164,796
Nevada	$276,209	Wisconsin	$156,312
New York	$19,243,893	Wyoming	$243,237
New Hampshire	$331,731	District of Columbia	$5,831,707
		Indiana Territory	$761,111

Status of Black Progress in 1897

There were 25,000 Black
school teachers in the United States.

* * * * *

There were 1,512,800 Black pupils in the
public schools. Plus, another 20,000
attending private schools, and 80,000 attending
mechanical or art institutions.

* * * * *

There were 63 Black Presidents of Negro Colleges.
Six hundred Blacks were members of the
Bar Association. Also, Deans in law colleges,
Court Commissioners and
many common Attorneys.

* * * * *

There were 1,000 graduates of
medical colleges and rising.

* * * * *

All the above from the book, "Sparkling Gems"

Chapter 8

PAST BLACK ROYALTY

Past Black Queen and Royalty of England

Is it important that the British know that their royal family has Black blood in its bloodline? We're sure they would want to suppress this information. As a matter of fact, in February of 1993, this information on the Black Kings and Queens of Europe was offered to a national magazine. They did not feel that there would be enough interest in the story for their readers; they turned it down. We feel it was just another tactic to suppress the information.

Queen Charlotte Sophia, consort of George III, by Ramsay, clearly shows a Negro strain. Horace Walpole, who saw her wrote of her, "nostril spreading too wide; mouth has the same fault." Queen Charlotte Sophia, was the grandmother of Queen Victoria and great-great grandmother of King George VI.

* * * * *

Queen Charlotte Sophia
Consort of George III and grandmother of Queen Victoria
From a portrait by Thomas Frye (1719-1762).

Charlotte Sophia, Queen of England

From Negro Slave to White English Royalty

1 Abraham Hannibal, “Negro of Peter the Great”
2 Admiral Ivan Hannibal, His Son
3 Pushkin, Great-Grandson of Hannibal
4 Marquess of Milford Haven, Descendant of Pushkin, Great-Grandson of Queen Victoria, Cousin of George VI and Best Man at the Wedding of Princess Elizabeth, Heiress to Britain’s Throne

Other Royalty

Regarding British Royalty, Professor Ben-Jochannan asserts that: "The Kings and Queens of Great Britain since George III have been descendants of this Negro."

Alessandro Dei Medici

Edward Scobie, Past Associate Professor of History, Black Studies Department, City College of New York and a visiting professor at Princeton, reminds us that:

> "Alessandro dei Medici, known as 'The Moor,' became the first Duke of Florence."
>
> "His mother was Black and had been in the service of the Pope's aunt, the wife of a mule driver. But Pope Clement VII, then Cardinal dei Medici, took her as his mistress, and was the father of Alessandro. All the writers of his time

stated that Alessandro was a mulatto, and his African features were vividly depicted by the paintings of Bronsini and Vasari."

For additional information read "SEX AND RACE."

Past Kings, Queens and Royalty of Sweden

When you think of Sweden, you think of the land of blond and blue-eyed people. Their blond and blue eyes are to represent the purest of the White race. Once again we prove there is Black blood in everyone's ancestors. It may not be as far back, as one might think.

Adolphus Gustavus IV, King of Sweden was said to have been and the son of Major Adolph Frederick Munck (of Finnish-Sweden Ancestry); with a Negro strain inherited from his maternal grandmother.

Gustavus III had been married for eleven years and had not consummated his marriage due to his sexual inability.

The ministers of Gustavus III were demanding an heir and the King promised them one. Major Munck was the King's most intimate friend so it was said the King requested Munck's aid. The King told the Queen of his dilemma and plans; she agreed. The King conducted Munck to the Queen and closed the door, leaving them there.

When the King's mother learned Queen Sophia was with child, she agitated openly and exposed her son's inability.

Read: "SEX AND RACE, VOL. 1," p. 192 and p. 298 (notes on illustrations)

Following Gustavus IV, John Baptiste Bernadottle, a colored man, ascended to the throne of Sweden in 1818, as Charles XIV.

Read: "100 AMAZING FACTS ABOUT THE NEGRO" p. 10 and 61

1 Count Munck von Fulkila
2 Gustavus IV, Adolphus, King of Sweden
3 Gustavus III
4 Queen Sophia of Sweden

A Few Past Great Kings and Queens of Africa

Nszingha
Queen of Matamba
West Africa (1582-1663)

Idris Alooma
SuHan of Bornu
(1580-1617)

Shamba Bolongongo
King of the Congo
(1600-1620)

Makeda
Queen of Sheba
Ethiopia (Abyssinia)
(960 B.C.)

Taharqu
King of Nubia
(710-664 B.C.)

Menelek II
King of Ethiopia
(Abyssinia)
Descendent of King Solomon
and Queen of Sheba (1844-1913)

Tehkamenin
King of Ghana
(1037-1075.)

Hannibal
Ruler of Carthage
(247-183 B.C.)

Mansa Kankan Mussa
King of Mali
(1306-1332)

Moshoeshoe
King of Basutoland
(1815-1868)

Affonso I
King of the Kongo
(1506-1540)

Khama
King of Bechuanaland
(1819-1923)

Shaka
King of the Zulus
(1818-1828)

Nandi
Queen of Zululand
(1778-1826)

Osei Tufu
King of Asante (Ghama)
(1680-1717)

Samory Toure
Black Napoleon of the
Sudan
(1830-1900)

Queen Amina of Zaria
(1588-1589)

Java
King of the Opobo
(Nigeria)
1821-1891)

Behanzia Hossu Bowelle
King Shark of Dahomeg
(1841-1906)

Sunni Ali Ber
King of Soughay (Suden)
(1493-1529)

Askia Muhammed Toure
King of Songhay
(1493-1529)

Hatshepsat
Queen of Far Antiquity
(1503-1482 B.C.)

Tiye
Nubian Queen of Egypt
(1415-1340 B.C.)

Nefertari Egypt
Nubian Queen of Egypt
(1292-1225 B.C.)

Cleopatra VII
Queen of Egypt
(69-30 B.C.)

Thutmose III
Pharoah of Egypt
(1504-1450 B.C.)

Akhenaton
Pharaoh of Egypt
(1375-1388 B.C.)

For more information see: The Budweiser Series "Past Kings and Queens Of Africa"

For additional kings and queens, see section in this book entitled, Black People / Black Nations of the Bible.

Some Present Traditional Rulers of Nigeria

During and right after the colonization of Nigeria, there were three main segments in Nigeria separated by the rivers Niger and Benue. Inside these segments, there are three main tribes, namely Ibo, Hausa and Yoruba. Each area has a tribal ruler who presides over the tribal population. These rulers wield immense influence on their subjects and show an aura of absolute majesty.

The Hausa Tribe, controls the North of Nigeria; the largest land area. Their ruler is Ado Bayero, "The Emir of Kano."

The Ibo Tribe, control the South East of Nigeria. Their ruler is Frederick Achebe, called "The Obi of Onitsha."

The Yoruba Tribe, occupies the South West area of Nigeria. Their ruler is Okunade Sijawade, Olubuse II, "The Oni of Ife." He is the head of the Yoruba Tribe around the world, and is considered as the "Black Pope."

There are many more traditional kings and rulers in Nigeria. We chose only to list the rulers from the three main sections. Africa contains many kings and queens.

Six Past Black Emperors of the Roman Empire

Have you ever heard of a Black Roman Emperor? I never heard of Black Cleopatra until a few years ago. How about Black Ludwig Von Beethoven? See picture below.

1. The Young Emperor Honorius
   (see picture following)

2. Septimus Severus

3. Firmus

4. Macrimus

5. Henry III, Emperor of the Holy Roman Empire (1013-56 AD) married the daughter of Canute, King of England

6. Theodosius the Great

Young Emperor Honorius,
After Jean Paul Laurens,
Distinguished French Painter

In reading the book references, listed at the back of this book, you understand why blacks were involved in all nations.

For Additional information read:

"SEX AND RACE, VOL. I"
"WHAT THEY NEVER TOLD YOU IN HISTORY CLASS"

Three Past Black Popes of the Catholic Church

As with most other information concerning Blacks involved in high positions, the Catholic Church has not done much to inform its members that there were Black popes among its early leaders.

The book, "From Peter to John Paul II," by Franklin Kern, page 272, listed Three Popes having come from Africa, however during the early years of Christianity, we know most Christian leaders were black and I'm sure there were many other Black Popes.

Taken from "What They Never Told You In History Class" by Indus Hamit Kush, page 93, quotes:

> The New York Voice (July 2, 1980) featured an article entitled, "Black Popes Played Strong Role in Christian History," written by Mark Hyman in which he reports that: Victor was the fifteenth pope and a native of Black Africa...he was buried near the body of Apostle Peter, the first pope in the Vatican.

1. Pope Victor I, 189-199
   Served during the reign of Emperor Septimus Severus, also an African, who had led Roman legions in Britain.

2. St. Melchiades (Miltiades)
   July 2, 311 - January 11, 314
   Miltiades led the church to final victory over the Roman Empire. Miltiades was buried on the famous Appian Way.

3. St. Gelasius I,
   March 1, 142 - November 21, 496
   Gelasius I, is said to have "delivered the city of Rome from the perils of famine."

For additional information read:

"SEX AND RACE"
"100 AMAZING FACTS ABOUT THE NEGRO"
"WHAT THEY NEVER TOLD YOU IN HISTORY CLASS"

* * * * *

Plagiarizing Greek Philosophers (Aristotle, Plato, Socrates, etc.)

For centuries, the White power structure has manipulated and covered up everything they could that indicated the intelligence and contributions to civilization by Black People. They have managed to hide the fact that civilization was started by Blacks.

"The land of the Blacks was not only the "cradle of civilization" itself, but Blacks were once the leading people on earth. Egypt once, was not only all Black, but the very name "Egypt" was derived from Blacks. Black People were the pioneers in science, medicine, architecture, writing and were the first builders in stone."

Dr. Chancellor Williams
"THE DESTRUCTION OF BLACK CIVILIZATION"

Characteristics of Greek Philosophy

"The term Greek Philosophy, to begin with a misnomer, for there is no such philosophy in existence originating from Ancient Greece. The ancient Greek philosophers stole what they learned from the ancient Egyptians. These ancient Egyptians developed a very complex religious system, called the Mysteries, which was also the first system of salvation.

"As such, it regarded the human body as a prison house of the soul, which could be liberated from its bodily impediments, through the disciplines of the Arts and Sciences, and advanced from the level of a mortal to that of a God. This was the notion of the summum bonum, of greatest good, to which all men must aspire, and it also became the basis of all ethical concepts. The Egyptian Mystery System was also a Secret Order and membership was gained by initiation and a pledge to secrecy. The teaching was graded and delivered orally to the Neophyte; and under these circumstances of secrecy, the Egyptians developed secret systems of writing and teaching, and forbade their Initiates from writing what they had learned.

"After nearly five thousand years of prohibition against the Greeks, they were permitted to enter Egypt for the purpose of their education. First through the Persian invasion and secondly through the invasion of Alexander the Great. From the sixth century B.C. therefore to the death of Aristotle (322 B.C.) the Greeks made the best of their chance to learn all they could about

> Egyptian culture; most students received instructions directly from the Egyptian Priest, but after the invasion by Alexander the Great, the Royal temples and libraries were plundered and pillaged, and Aristotle's school converted the library at Alexandria into a research center. There is no wonder then, that the production of the unusually large number of books ascribed to Aristotle has proved a physical impossibility, for any single man within a life time."

Taken from

"STOLEN LEGACY," Introduction, p. 1
by George G.M. James

* * * * *

One day while on my way to the British Museum in London, I stopped by an Egyptian Book Store in search of some books on Black Egypt. The clerk stated she had none, however I might be interested in a book that was very controversial. The book she sold me was titled "Black Athena" by Martin Bernal.

Writing from "Black Athena"

What is classical about Classical Civilization? In one of the most audacious works of scholarship ever written, Martin Bernal challenges the whole basis of our thinking about the question.

> "Classical civilization," he argues, "has deep roots in Afro-Asiatic cultures. But these Afro-Asiatic influences have been systematically ignored,

denied or suppressed since the eighteenth century, chiefly for racist reasons.

"According to the view in which most of us have been brought up, Greek civilization was the result of the conquest of sophisticated but weak native population by vigorous Indo-European speakers – or Aryans – from the north. Out the Classical Greeks themselves, Professor Bernal argues, knew nothing about this "Aryan Model: Although proud of themselves and their recent accomplishments, they did not see their political institutions, science, philosophy or religion as original. They derived them...from the East in general, and Egypt in particular."

"BLACK ATHENA" by Martin Bernal

* * * * *

Another Surprise !

Black Beethoven

Ludwig Van Beethoven was described as a Dark Mulatto. He was called, "The Black Spaniard." Joseph Haydn, his teacher, was a "Moor." The name "Moor" meaning Negro, in all the countries of the Western world.

Taken from "SEX AND RACE"

Ludwig von Beethoven, At the Age of 44
Drawn from Life by Letronne
Engraved by Hofel

Chapter 9

BLACK STATUE OF LIBERTY

The people of France did not agree with slavery. In 1865, a Frenchmen by the name of Edward Rene Liefevre de Laboulaye wanted to create a monument to honor the freedom of the Africans in America.

Mr. De Laboulaye was President of the French Antislavery Society in 1865, and was impressed by the determinations of the Africans to be free.

A friend of Mr. De Laboulave, Auguste Bartholdi, had gone to Egypt and was awed by the great monuments and statues of Africans in the Nile Valle, (ancient Kemet), he and de Laboulaye conceived the idea to create a large statue of liberty, of a Black woman with a spiked crown, a broken chain in her lowered left hand, and another chain at her bare feet, to symbolize her freedom from slavery, and the victory of African people over their enslavement. There were a half-million slaves fighting in the Civil War, causing the defeat of the South.

When the statue was presented to the U.S. Minister to France in 1884, it is said that he remonstrated that the dominate view of the broken shackles would be offensive to a United States South since the statue would be a reminder of Blacks winning their freedom. It would be a reminder to a beaten South of the ones who caused their defeat; their despised former captives.

The statue had characteristics of Negroid features, full lips, round face, wide nose, totally different from the European face that is profiled on the current monument.

When the original concept was presented to the American Committee of the Statue of Liberty in New York. The statue was rejected.

It is reported that the final version was modeled after Bartholdi's mother. The chain in her left hand was replaced by a tablet marked "4th July 1776," the chain at her feet was replaced by sandals with an unspiked crown.

As other things in history have been distorted and covered up, so has the Black Statue of Liberty. The United States government does not want the world to know the true meaning of the Statue of Liberty.

Dr. Leonard Jefferies, Chairman of the Department of Africana Studies at the City College of New York has said, "Several of these original models featuring a Black Woman are in the New York City Museum but are locked away and hidden from public viewing."

We found out about the Black statue from an Internet posting which listed where the proof could be found. The Internet listing read:

1. You may go and see the original model of the Statue of Liberty, with broken chain at her left foot and in her left hand, at the New York City Museum (Fifth Avenue and 103rd Street). Call (212) 534-1672 or call the same number and dial extension 208,

A Black Statue of Liberty - Artist's Concept
Drawn by Juanita Davis

ask to speak to Peter Simmons. He can send you some documentation.

2. Check with the New York Times magazine, Part II, May 18,1986. The dark original face of the Statue can be seen in the New York Post, June 17, 1986. Also, the Post stated the reason for the broken chains at her feet.

3. Finally, you may check with the French Mission or the French Embassy at the United Nations or in Washington, D.C. Ask for some original French material on the Statue of Liberty including the Bartholdi original model. You can call in September (202) 944-6060 or 6400.

Note! We tried:

1. Called to speak to Peter Simmons. We were told Simmons no longer worked there; they knew nothing about the Black Statue. I wonder why Mr. Simmons no longer works there.

2. There was no copy of the New York Post, June 17, 1986 issue in the Main Library in Los Angeles, California.

3. We called the French Embassy four times. They said they would send us the information. We have not received anything from them. Sooner or later, things done in the dark will come out in the light.

Having been unsuccessful in getting a copy of the original Black Statue of Liberty, we decided to have an artist draw their concept of the Black Statue, according to the description.

* * * * *

ILLUSION

SOMETIMES LIFE
CAN BE AN ILLUSION.
FOR EVERYTHING YOU SEE,
MAY NOT BE
WHAT YOU PERCEIVE IT TO BE.

Chapter 10

BLACK INTELLIGENCE

In every field there is a Black at or near the top. If one were to truly measure intelligence of a race, they would have to evaluate what the race, as a whole, has done. You must remember that while the Black man built this country, the White man was sitting on his horse with a whip, or he was sitting on the porch sipping his drink. History books have excluded the true contributions of Black People and their creation of civilization, cities and all arts and sciences. You are now learning the truth. When the White man was semi-savage, Black People were studying arts and sciences. This is a fact!

Read "The Moors" in this chapter.

Millions of dollars have been spent over the years, with different studies, trying to prove that Blacks are intellectually inferior to Whites and other races. The Bell Curve was a study designed to prove the inferiority of Black intelligence, however, it does not appear the writers did a good job in their research, because they did not evaluate the amount of intelligence it took to invent every thing listed below and achieve the high positions that Black People have held throughout history.

Read the story below "If There Were No Black People in the World"

White people say anything they want and expect Black People to accept it with a smile. The late William K. Coors, Chairman of Adolph Brewing Company reportedly told a group of minority business owners attending a seminar:

> "It's not that the dedication is less. In fact, it's greater. They lack the intellectual capacity to succeed, and it's taking them down the tubes, one of the best things (slave traders) did for you was to drag your ancestors over here in chains."

Jet Magazine, April 19, 1984

* * * * *

Even one of Richard Nixon's top advisors, John D. Ehrlichman, repeated a belief expressed by Richard Nixon.

> "America's Blacks could only marginally benefit from federal programs because Blacks are genetically inferior to Whites."

New York Times, Friday, December 11, 1981

* * * * *

A Ronald Reagan appointee, Mele Hall, proclaimed that,

> "Black and brown people are culturally or even genetically inferior. They have been conditioned," she said, "by 10,000 years of selective breeding for personal combat and the anti-work ethic of jungle freedoms" and were therefore unfit for civic life."

Covert Action, Winter 1992-93, p. 31

Excerpts from

"A Report From the Center for The Study of Psychiatry"

September 23, 1992

The Federal Violence Initiative

One of the government's highest ranking psychiatrists, Dr. Frederick Goodwin, presented the Violence Initiative to the National Mental Health Advisory Council on February 11, 1992. This research compared violent inner city youth to rhesus monkeys that only want to kill each other; have sex and reproduce. His observations drew upon ongoing federal research comparing violent rhesus monkeys to problem children in regard to genetic factors, biochemical imbalances and drug treatment.

According to Goodwin, the violence initiative will become fully operational in 1994 when it is presented to Congress as the government's number one mental health funding priority.

The Federal Violence Initiative required teachers to identify 12-15% of the students in each classroom with behavior problems and subject the students to behavior modification drugs (such as Ritalin) without parent consent. The program led to abusive practices, such as pressuring and forcing parents to drug their children with drugs.

THIS IS AMERICA

"... instead of waiting to execute degenerate offspring for crimes ... , society can prevent those who are manifestly unfit from continuing their kind."

U.S. Supreme Court, 1927

* * * * *

"Neurosurgeon William Sweet testified in 1968 before the New York State Legislature that those participating in urban uprising were suffering from brain disease (psychomotor epilepsy); i.e., Blacks who rebelled against their plight could be "cured" by carving their brains or drugging them."

"That same year, "successful" psychosurgery was performed on California prisoners and other "undesirables." Dr. Jewell Osterholm and his associate, Dr. David Matthews, confessed to performing psychosurgery, or cingulotomies, on drug addicts, alcoholics, and "neurotics." According to Dr. Peter Breggin, "a cingulomy is nothing more than the newest version of lobotomy. It can turn a person into a zombie. It makes the patient docile, subdued and easy to manage." This later description was precisely what certain United States elites desired for often-rebellious Blacks."

From Covert Action, Winter 1992-1993, page 31

In every field there are Blacks at the top. So much for the junk in the bell curve. Below we mention a few Black doctors that are among the best in the world. Remember, this book only touch on the millions of high Black achievers. Look at the Black Inventions below, then search out other books on Black progress.

Dr. Benjamin S. Carson, Sr. headed the first surgical team that successfully separated a pair of Siamese twins, who were born joined together at the head. Dr. Carson, specializes in pediatric neurosurgery. In 1984, Dr. Carson became Director of Pediatric Neurosurgery at John Hopkins Hospital; the youngest doctor to hold that position. He has received numerous awards for his pioneering role and for the development of brain surgery techniques.

Dr. Keith Lanier Black, head of the Comprehensive Brain Tumor Program at Cedars-Sinai Medical Center in Los Angeles, California. Dr. Black is considered one of the foremost Neurosurgeons and researchers in his field, in the United States. He has published over 100 scientific papers. In 1994, he patented his method of selective opening of abnormal brain tissue capillaries. Dr. Black is best known for his discovery that bradykinin, a peptide occurring naturally in the body, was highly effective in opening the blood-brain barrier by causing capillary walls to be leaky. The blood-brain barrier is a protective network of blood vessels which impedes the progress of medication moving from the blood stream to brain tissue.

Patients from all over the world, many who have been told there is no hope, come to see Dr. Black at Cedars

Sinai Hospital in Los Angeles. Dr. Black says, "With each patient you see, you give a little bit of your soul. It's the power of touch, the power of healing that goes beyond just doing the surgery and giving the medicine."

Dr. Daniel Hale Williams was the first doctor to perform a successful open-heart surgery. In 1856, he was one of the founders of Provident Hospital in Chicago.

Dr. Sylvester Gates is a renowned physicist. Gates is not only at the forefront of revisionist physics, but he is also in front of a window looking out on the rebuilding and regeneration of physics at Howard University, the establishment of a scientific beachhead that will take the institution into the next century of technology.

Gates directs the Center for the Study of Terrestrial and Extraterrestrial Atmospheres (CSTEA), an interdisciplinary research unit funded by a $5 million National Aeronautics and Space Administration grant at Howard University.

Since the eighties, scientists have redefined how they look at the universe – redefined it so that both Einstein's theory of relativity and the classical laws of physics formulated by Sir Isaac Newton ... well, they are being turned on their ears.

Dr. Gates says, "It's really funny to think, that I'm working on the same stuff that Einstein did. It's odd – I'm correcting Einstein. I'm beyond Einstein." At the forefront of Gate's work are the theories of super symmetry and super strings.

You don't have to be Einstein to know that two objects can't occupy the same space at the same time. According to the laws of the universe as we know it, and in particular, a concept called the Pauli Exclusion Principle, it just isn't possible, right? Wrong.

Dr. Gates holds an imaginary flashlight in each hand. He turns them on so that their rays pour through each other. "So you see," he says, "that photons don't obey the exclusion principle because they are occupying the same space. The light rays of the flashlights flow through each other."

Gates received the Martin Luther King, Jr. Award for his contributions to the education of minority students at the Massachusetts Institute of Technology.

Dr. Mark Dean is an IBM Scientist who co-invented, with Dennis Moeller, the improvements in computer architecture that allow IBM and compatible PC's to use high performance software and to work in tandem with peripheral devices. The work allows IBM and IBM compatible computer components to communicate with each other in a high-speed and efficient manner. The first commercial use of this development was marketed in 1984 in the IBM PC/AT, and it is currently being used in more than 40 million personal computers produced each year.

Dr. Dean has been with IBM since 1980, and was named an IBM Fellow in 1995, one of only 50 active fellows of IBM's 200,000 employees. Dean was the first and only African American to be honored with an IBM Fellowship. He is currently Vice-President of Performance for the RS/6000 Division in Austin, Texas.

Dean holds more than 20 United States Patents, including three of IBM's original nine PC patents.

Dr Dean was inducted into the National Inventors Hall of Fame. He joins the ranks of Thomas Edison, Henry Ford, Louis Pasteur, George Eastman and Charles Goodyear. Only 134 other men and women are honored in the Inventor's Hall of Fame.

Henry Thomas Sampson invented the cellular phone on July 6, 1971. His awards and honors include: Fellow of United States Navy, 1962-1964; Atomic Energy Commission, 1964-1967; Black Image Award from Aerospace Corp., 1982; Blacks in Engineering, Applied Science, and Education Award, Los Angeles Council of Black Professional Engineers, 1983.

Otis Boykin is an inventor. Among his inventions was an electrical device that is utilized in all guided missiles and all IBM computers. He also invented controls for the Pacemaker.

Colonel Frederick Gregory was the first Black astronaut pilot. He also redesigned the cockpits for space shuttles. Dr. Gregory was also on the team that pioneered the microwave instrumentation landing system. Bendix Aircraft Company will be promoting this system worldwide to land planes without a pilot, using this computer-based microwave system.

Dr. J. Earnest Wilkins and Lloyd Quartman were among the six Black scientists who helped in the making of the first atomic bomb (code named the Manhattan Project).

Lloyd Quartman also helped develop the first nuclear reactor, which was used in the atomic powered submarine called the Nautilus.

We recommend reading:

"BLACK SCIENTISTS OF AMERICA"
by Richard X. Donovan

* * * * *

"WHEN BLACKS WERE STUDYING AND DEVELOPING ARTS AND SCIENCES . . . EUROPEANS WERE CAVE PEOPLE"

"The accident of the predominance of White men in modern times should not give us supercilious ideas about color or persuade us to listen to superficial theories about the innate superiority of the White-skinned man.

"Four thousand years ago, when civilization was already one or two thousand years old, White men were just a bunch of semi-savages on the outskirts of the civilized world. If there had been anthropologists in Crete, Egypt, and Babylonia, they would have pronounced the White race obviously inferior and might have discoursed learnedly on the superior germ-plasm or glands of colored folk."

Quote of Joseph McCabe, taken from
"Ethiopia and the Origin of Civilization"
by John C. Jackson

* * * * *

"For the first two or three thousand years of civilization, there was not a civilized White men on earth. Civilization was founded and developed by the swarthy races of Mesopotamia, Syria and Egypt, while the White race remained so barbaric that in those days an Egyptian or Babylonian priest would have said, "The riffraff of White tribes a few hundred miles to the north of their civilization were hopelessly incapable of acquiring the knowledge requisite to progress."

Read: "THE BANKRUPTCY OF CHRISTIAN SUPERNATURALISM, VOL. II," p. 19
by Bishop William Montgomery Brown

* * * * *

The Moors

(Moors was the name Europeans gave to Black People; such as Negro used in America).

During the European Dark Ages, between the 7th and 14th centuries AD, the Moorish Empire in Spain became one of the world's finest civilizations. General Tarik, and his Black Moorish army from Morocco, conquered Spain after a weeklong battle with King Roderick in 711 AD. (The word tariff and the Rock of Gibraltar were named after him). They found that Europe, with the assistance of the Catholic Church, had returned almost to complete barbarism. The population was 90% illiterate and had lost all of the civilizing principles that were passed on by the ancient Greeks and Romans.

The Moors reintroduced mathematics, medicine, agriculture, and the physical sciences. The Moorish craftsman also produced world class glass, pottery, vases, mosaics, and jewelry.

The Moors introduced to Europe paved, lighted streets with raised sidewalks for pedestrians, flanked by uninterrupted rows of buildings. Paved and lighted streets did not appear in London or Paris for hundreds of years. They constructed thousands of public markets and mills in each city. Cordova alone had 5,000 of each. They also introduced to Spain underwear and bathing with soap. Their public baths numbered in the thousands when bathing in the rest of Europe was frowned upon as a diabolical custom to be avoided by all good Christians. Poor hygiene contributed to the plagues in the rest of Europe.

Moorish monarchs dwelled in sumptuous palaces while the crowned heads of England, France, and Germany lived in barns that lacked windows, toilet, and chimneys, and with only a hole in the roof as the exit for smoke. Human waste material was thrown in the streets since no bathrooms were present.

Education was made mandatory by the Moors, while 90% of Europe was illiterate, including the kings and queens. The Moors introduced public libraries to Europe with 600,000 books housed in Cordova alone. They established 17 outstanding universities in Spain. Since Africa is a matriarchal society, women were also encouraged to devote themselves to serious study, and it was only in Spain that one could find female doctors, lawyers, and scientists.

One of the worst mistakes the Moors made was to introduce gunpowder technology from China into Europe because their enemies adopted this weapon and used it to drive them out of Spain. Europe then took the 700 years of civilization and education re-taught to them by the Moors and used this knowledge to attack Africa. While the Moors were re-civilizing Europe, great empires were thriving in Western Africa and frequently traded with the Moors.

Taken from "BLACK PEOPLE & THEIR PLACE IN HISTORY." Read the total story.

"If There Were No Black People In The World" . . .

A Story

This is a story of a little boy name Theo, who woke up one morning and asked God, "What if there were no Black People in the world?'

Well, God thought about that for a moment and then said, 'Son, follow me around today and let's just see what it would be like if there were no Black People in the world. Get dressed and we will get started."

Theo ran to his room to put on his clothes and shoes, but there were no shoes, and his clothes were all wrinkled. He looked for the iron, but when he reached for the ironing board, it was no longer there. You see Sarah Boone, a Black woman, invented the ironing board and Jan E. Matzellinger, a Black man, invented the shoe lasting machine.

"Oh well," God said, "Go and do your hair."

Theo ran in his room to comb his hair, but the comb was not there. You see, Walter Sammons, a Black man, invented the comb. Theo decided to just brush his hair, but the brush was gone. You see, Lydia O. Newman, a Black female invented the brush.

Well, he was a sight, no shoes, wrinkled clothes, hair a mess without the hair inventions of Madam C. J. Walker . . . . well, you get the picture.

God told Theo, "Let's do the chores around the house and then take a trip to the grocery store."

Theo's job was to sweep the floor. He swept and swept and swept. When he reached for the dustpan, it was not there. You see, Lloyd P. Ray, a Black man, invented the dustpan. So he swept his pile of dirt over in the corner and left it there. He then decided to mop the floor, but the mop was gone. You see, Thomas W. Stewart, a Black man, invented the mop.

Theo thought to himself, "I'm not having any luck."

"Well, son," God said. "We should wash the clothes and prepare a list for the grocery store."

When he was finished, Theo went to place the clothes in the dryer, but it was not there. You see, George T. Samon, a Black man, invented the clothes dryer.

Theo got a pencil and some paper to prepare the list for the market, but noticed that the pencil lead was broken, well he was out of luck because John Love, a Black man, invented the pencil sharpener. He reached for a pen, but it was not there because William Purvis, a Black man, invented the fountain pen. As a matter of fact, Lee Burridge invented the typewriting machine and W.A. Lavette, the printing press.

So they decided to head out to the market. Well, when Theo opened the door, he noticed the grass was as high as he was tall. You see the lawn mower was invented by John Burr, a Black man.

They made their way over to the car and found that it just wouldn't go. You see, Robert Spikes, a Black man, invented the automatic gearshift and Joseph Gammel invented the supercharge for internal combustion engines.

Elevator
A. Miles
October 27, 1891

Electric Lamp
Lewis Latimer
March 21, 1882

Fire Extinguisher
T. Marshall
May 26, 1872

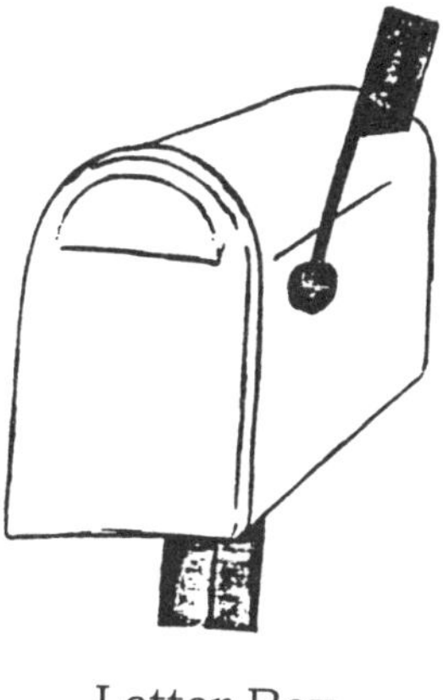

Letter Box
P. Downing
October 27, 1891

They noticed that the few cars that were moving were running into each other and having wrecks because there were no traffic signals. You see, Garrett A. Morgan, a Black man invented the traffic light.

Well, it was getting late, so they walked to the market, got their groceries and returned home. Just when they were about to put away the milk, eggs and butter, they noticed the refrigerator was gone. You see John Standard, a Black man, invented the refrigerator. So they put the food on the counter. By this time, they noticed it was getting mighty cold. Theo went to turn up the heat and what do you know, Alice Parker, a Black female, invented the heating furnace.

Even in the summer time they would have been out of luck because Frederick Jones, a Black man, invented the air conditioner.

It was almost time for Theo's father to arrive home. He usually took the bus, but there was no bus because its precursor was the electric trolley, invented by another Black man, Elbert T. Robinson. He usually took the elevator from his office on the 20th floor, but there was no elevator because Alexander Miles, a Black man, invented the elevator. He usually dropped off the office mail at a nearby mailbox, but it was no longer there because Phillip Downing, a Black man, invented the letter drop mailbox and William Barry invented canceling machine.

Theo sat at the kitchen table with his head in his hands. When his father arrived he asked, "Why are you sitting in the dark?" Why? Because Lewis Howard Latimer, a Black man, invented the filament within the light bulb.

Theo quickly learned what it would be like if there were no Black People in the world. Not to mention if he were ever sick and needed blood. Charles Drew, a Black scientist, found a way to preserve and store blood, which led to his starting the world's first blood bank. And what if a family member had to have heart surgery. This would not have been possible without Dr. Daniel Hale Williams, a Black doctor, who performed the first open-heart surgery.

So if you ever wonder, like Theo, where we would be without Blacks? Well, it's pretty plain to see, we could very well still be in the dark !!!

Received from the Internet
No Copyright or Author Noted
Posted in the Interest of Black People's Education

* * * * *

"Think About This" . . . Another Story

A very humorous and revealing story is told about a group of White people who were fed up with African Americans, so they joined together and wished themselves away. They passed through a deep dark tunnel and emerged in sort of a twilight zone where there is an America without Black People. At first these White people breathed a sigh of relief. At last, they say, no more crime, drugs, violence and welfare. All of the Blacks have gone!! Then suddenly, reality sets in. The "New America" is not America at all – only a barren land. There are very few crops that have flourished because the nation was built on a slave- supported system.

There are no cities with tall skyscrapers because Alexander Mils, a Black man, invented the elevator, and without it one finds great difficulty reaching high floors. There are few if any cars because Richard Spikes, a Black man, invented the automatic gearshift, Joseph Gammell, also Black, invented the Super Charge System for Internal Combustion Engines, and Garrett A. Morgan invented the traffic signals.

Furthermore, one could not use the rapid transit system because its precursor was the electric trolley, which was invented by another Black man Elbert R. Robinson.

Even if there were streets on which cars and a rapid transit system could operate, they were cluttered with paper because an African American, Charles Brooks, invented the street sweeper.

There were few, if any, newspapers, magazines and books because John Love invented the pencil sharpener, William Purvis invented the fountain pen, Lee Burridge invented the typewriting machine and W.A. Lovette invented the advanced printing press. They were all Black.

Even if Americans could write their letters, articles and books, they would not have been transported by mail because William Barry invented the postmarking and canceling machine, William Purvis invented the hand stamp and Philip Downing invented the letter drop.

The lawns were brown and wilted because Joseph Smith invented the lawn sprinkler and John Burr the lawn mower.

When they entered their homes, they found them to be

poorly ventilated and poorly heated. You see, Frederick Jones invented the air conditioner and Alice Parker the heating furnace. Their homes were also dim. But of course, Lewis Latimer invented the electric lamp, Michael Harvey invented the lantern and Granville T. Woods invented the Automatic Cut off Switch. Their homes were also filthy because Thomas W. Steward invented the mop and Lloyd P. Ray, the dustpan.

Their children met them at the door barefooted, shabby, motley and unkempt. But what could one expect. Jan E. Matzelinger invented the shoe-lasting machine, Walter Sammons invented the comb, Sarah Boone invented the ironing board and George T. Samon invented the clothes dryer.

Finally, they were resigned to at least having dinner amidst all of this turmoil. But here again, the food had spoiled because another Black man John Standard invented the refrigerator. What would this world be like without the contributions of Black People?

Received from the Internet
No Copyright or Author Noted
Posted in the Interest of Black People's Education

* * * * *

"Black for 5 Minutes" . . . Another Story

A little White boy was watching his mother in the kitchen make a chocolate cake from scratch. While the mother had her head turned, the little White boy went to the table, dipped both hands in the chocolate frosting and covered his face with it.

The mother turned around to see what the boy was doing and said, "Boy, what the hell are you doing?"

The son gleefully replied "Look, Mama! I'm Black!!"

The mother became enraged and slapped the crap out of her son. She then said, "Boy, go show your father what you've done!"

The boy then walked in to the den where his father was reading and said, "Look Daddy! I'm Black!!"

The father put his magazine down and had a very puzzled look on his face from seeing the chocolate on the boy's face. The father said, "Come here, boy!" The boy came to him and the fathered smacked the wine out of his son. The father angrily said, "Now go show your grandpa what you've done!!!"

The boy then slowly walked to his grandpa who was on the porch and said, "Um...Grandpa. Look what I did. I'm Black now." The grandfather said gruffly "COME HERE BOY!" The grandfather took to boy over his knee and proceeded to spank him. "That'll teach you! Now go back in the kitchen with your Mama!!"

The boy walks back in the kitchen and mother said, "I hope you've learned your lesson, young man!"

The boy says with a scowl on his face, "Heck yeah! I've been Black for 5 minutes and I hate you White bastards already!"

Received from the Internet
No Copyright or Author Noted
Posted in the Interest of Black People's Education

Chapter 11

BLACK INVENTIONS

A Major Force in the Industrial Revolution

Having taken almost everything from the Black Man, can you imagine the White Man giving credit to the Black Man for inventions; especially if he does not have to?

We believe that of the listed patents by Black People during the 19th Century, Blacks only received credit for 25%. The rest were taken, stolen or purchased for little money. Look at the spark plug and traffic light. How about the cellular phone, which is now used all over the world? Could those inventors have gone to the bank like Bill Gates? These are just a few of the many Black inventions used every day, however those inventors were not able to reap the financial rewards they should have.

One of the major cover-ups in history was the fact that Black People, brought to America to be enslaved, were not, "savages." There were master craftsmen, scientist, doctors, architect, etc., captured to build America.

* * * * *

Dr. Robert I. Rothberg of Harvard clarifies why so many Blacks, supposedly one step from savagery, could produce so much, so soon and of such a sophisticated nature. In his authoritative, "POLITICAL HISTORY OF TROPICAL AFRICA," Professor Rothberg (like Life Magazine in its series on Black History) makes it very plain: "We may no longer assume that the 15th century

European found an Africa living in barbarism and slavery."

> "Much of the factual material was omitted from American texts to protect the conscience of those who had built their economic citadels upon the traffic in slavery. Until now, there has been a wall of silence concerning the African civil service, postal systems, iron workers, shipbuilders, armorers, universities, astronomers, mathematicians, etc."

Taken from "BLACK INVENTORS OF AMERICA"

Benjamin Banneker

At the age of 5, Benjamin Banneker was considered a genius. He was also a brilliant mathematician and one of the six-man team appointed by George Washington to lay out the plans for the city of Washington D.C. After they laid out the blue prints for the city, the chairman, Major L'Enfant, abruptly resigned and returned to France with the plans for the city. Banneker's photographic memory enabled him to reproduce them in their entirety.

Banneker also invented the first clock constructed from America parts. He was an astronomer, and for decades published an Almanac & Ephemeris. For additional information see: Black Scientists of America, National Book Company, 1990.

In more recent times, among the designers of the Los Angeles Airport was a Black architect named Paul Williams. I wonder why this is not taught in Los Angeles schools!

These Are the Facts:

There is nothing in this world that moves by machine, (i.e., auto, airplane, boat or trains; no home, building, factory or industry that operates without an invention from a Black inventor.

It is impossible for any person to not utilize something everyday of their life, that was invented by a Black person.

The following are examples to back up our statement. The below inventions are only a few that Blacks received credit for.

Traffic Light
Garrett Morgan
November 20, 1923

Gas Mask
Garrett Morgan
October 13, 1914

SOME BLACK INVENTIONS

Invention	Inventor	Date	Patent No.
Airplane			
Aeroplane	William Hale	11-25-1925	1,563,278
Airplane Propeller	James S. Adams		
Air Ship (Blimp)	J.F. Pickering	02-20-1900	643,975
Flip Wing Plane	Herman Grimes		
Tires for Moon Buggie	Robert Shurney		
Helicopter Cockpit	Paul E. Williams		
Cockpit, Redesigned for Space Shuttle	Colonel Frederick Gregory		
Agricultural			
Bailing Press	J. Ross	09-05-1899	632,539
Churn	A.C. Richardson	02-17-1891	466,470
Combined Furrow Opener Stalk-Knocker	G.W. Murray	04-10-1894	517,960
Cotton Chopper	G.W. Murray	06-05-1894	520,888
Cultivator and Marker	G.W. Murray	04-10-1894	517,961
Fertilizer Distributor	G.W. Murray	06-05-1894	520,889

Invention	Inventor	Date	Patent No.
Ore Bucket	J.A. Joyce	04-26-1898	603,143
Planter	G.W. Murray	06-05-1894	520,887
Portable Weighing Scales	J.H. Hunter	11-03-1896	570,533
Accurate Weather Forecasting	Philip Emeagwali	1990	
Cattle Roping Apparatus	Darryle Thomas		
Corn Silkier	R.P. Scott	1894	
Machine For Cleaning Seed Cotton	Peter Walker	02-16-1897	577,153
Improved Petroleum Recovery	Philip Emeagwali	1990	
Mechanical Corn Planter	Henry Blair	10-14-1834	
Mechanical Seed Planter	Henry Blair	1830	
Mechanical Cotton Planter	Henry Blair	08-31-1836	
Refining Of Coconut Oil	A.P. Abourne	07-27-1980	230,518
Sugar Refining System	Norbett Rillieux	12-10-1846	4,879

Invention	Inventor	Date	Patent No.
Buildings			
Elevator	A. Miles	10-11-1887	371,207
Elevator Device	J. Cooper	04-02-1895	536,605
Fire Escape Bracket	C.V. Richey	12-28-1897	596,427
Fire Extinguisher	T.J. Marshall	05-26-1872	125,063
Portable Fire Escape	D. Mc Cree	11-11-1890	440,322
Fire Escape Ladder	J.B. Winters		
Automobile			
Starter Generator	F.M. Jones	07-12-1949	2,475,842
Engine Lubricators	E.J. McCoy	05-27-1873	139,407
Engine Lubricators	E.J. McCoy	03-28-1882	255,443
Two-Cycle Gasoline Engine	F.M. Jones	05-29-1945	2,376,968
Two-Cycle Gasoline Engine	F.M. Jones	11-28-1950	2,523,273
Automatic Air Brake	G.T. Woods	06-10-1902	701,981
Rotary Engine	A.J. Beard	07-05-1892	478,271
Automatic Gear Shift	R.B. Spikes	12-06-1932	1,889,814

Invention	Inventor	Date	Patent No.
Control Device For Internal Combustion Engines	F.M. Jones	09-02-1958	2,850,001
Automatic Traffic Signal	Garret A. Morgan	1925	
Means for Automatically Stopping and Starting Gas Engines	F.M. Jones	12-21-1943	2,337,164
Lubricator Safety Valves	E.J. McCoy	05-24-1887	363,529
Oil Cup	E.J. McCoy	11-15-1898	614,307
Exhaust Purifier	Rufus Stokes	04-16-1968	3,378,241
Motor	J. Gregory	04-26-1887	361,937
Velocipede	Matthew A. Cherry	05-08-1888	382,351
Spark Plugs	Edmond Berger		
Supercharge System for Internal Combustion Engine	Joseph Gammed		
T-Top Roof Cover	Natalie R. Love	05-05-1992	5,110,178
Tires Used on Moon Buggy	Robert Shurney		
Valves For Steam Engine	Frank J. Ferrell	1890-1893	

Invention	Inventor	Date	Patent No.
Inner Tube	David Boker		
Auto Seat Bed	Charles Bryant		
Vehicle Dash	Charles Patterson		
	Electrical		
Cellular Phone	Henry Thomas Sampson	07-06-1971	3,591,860
Gamma-Electric Cell	Henry Thomas Sampson and George H. Miley		
Electrical Cut-Off	G.T. Woods	04-23-1895	537,968
Programmable Remote Control	Joseph N. Jackson	03-28-1978 10-14-1980	4,081,754 4,228,543
Apparatus and Method Method of Providing Controller for Selective Blocking of Cable TV Programming.	Joseph N. Jackson	07-25-2002	6,094,194
Attachment For Shuttle Arm Device to Capture Satellites	William Harwell		
Multiplex Telegraph System (Allowed messages to be sent and received from moving trains)	Granville Woods	11-15-1887	
Hyperball Computer	Philip Emeagwali	04-00-1996	

Invention	Inventor	Date	Patent No.
Telephone	Granville Woods	10-11-1887	371,241
(His telephone was superior to Alexander Graham Bell's)			
World's Fastest Computer	Philip Emeagwali	1989	
Electrical Device Used in All Guided Missiles and All IBM Computers	Otis Boykin		
Entertainment			
Guitar	R.F. Flemming, Jr.	03-03-1886	338,727
Player Piano	Joseph H. Dickson	06-11-1912	1,028,996
Keyboard Stand	Joanna Hardin	02-23-1993	5,188,321
Equipment			
Saw Attachment	Henry C. Webb	10-04-1892	483,971
Casket Lowering Device	A.C. Richardson	11-13-1894	529,311
Exhaust Purifier	Rufus Stokes	04-06-1968	3,378,241
Automatic Traffic Signal	Garret A. Morgan	1925	

Invention	Inventor	Date	Patent No.
Automatic Shoe Making Machine	Jan Matzelinger	1883	
Fabrication of Spectrometer	George Alcorn	10-21-1986	
Postmarking and Canceling Machine	William Barry		
Ship Propeller	George Tolivar	04-28-1891	451,086
Steam Table	G.W. Kelley	1897	
Street Sweeper	C.B. Brook	1896	
Wrench	Jack Johnson	04-18-1922	1,413,121
Nailing Machine	Jan E. Matzeliger	02-25-1896	421,954
	Health		
Chemical Compound to Preserve Meat	Lloyd A. Hall		
Discovered Compound in Cannabis to Cure Glaucoma	Manley West	1980-1987	
Laserphacoprobe	Patricia E. Bath, M.D.		
(Patented surgical laser device to remove cataracts)			

Invention	Inventor	Date	Patent No.
Invented Blood Banks	Dr. Charles Drew	1940	
(Established them around the world			
Medicine Tray	Joan Clark	1987	
Performed First Open Heart Surgery	Dr. Daniel Hale Williams	1893	
Small Pox Inoculation	Onesimus	1721	
(He brought this method from African where advanced medical practices were in use long before Europeans had any medical knowledge)			
Apparatus and Method Of Providing a Personal Fertility Predictor	Joseph N. Jackson	11-17-1998	5,836,890 6,022,323

Home

Invention	Inventor	Date	Patent No.
Air Conditioning Unit	F.M. Jones	07-12-1949	2,475,841
Biscuit Cutter	A.P. Ashbourne	11-30-1875	170,460
Bottle	A.C. Richardson	12-12-1899	638,811
Caps for Bottles	Jones & Nichols	09-13-1898	610,715
Cell Phones	Henry Sampson	07-06-1971	3,591,860
Clothes Dryer	George T. Samon	06-07-1892	476,416
Clothes Wringer	Ellen Elgin	1880	

Invention	Inventor	Date	Patent No.
Chamber Commode	Thomas Elkins	01-09-1892	122,518
Convertible Settee (Large sofa)	J.H. White	1892	
Corner Cleaner Attachment	Gertrude E. Downing and William Desjardin	02-13-1973	3,715,722
Curtain Rod	S.R. Scottron	08-30-1892	356,852
Curtain Rod Support	W.S. Grant	08-04-1896	565,075
Door Knob	O. Dorsey		
Dough Kneader	J.W. Reed	09-02-1884	304,552
Dustpan	Lloyd P. Ray		
Egg Beater	Willis Johnson	02-05-1884	292,821
Electric Lamp	Joseph V. Nichols	09-13-1881	247,097
	Lewis Latimer		
Fireplace Damper Actuating Tool	Virgie M. Ammons	09-30-1975	3,908,633
Folding Bed	L.C. Bailey	07-18-1899	629,286
Fruit Press	Madeline M. Turner	1916	
Gas Burner	Benjamin F. Jackson	04-04-1899	622,482
Gridiron	J. Hawkins	03-26-1845	3,973
Heating Furnace	Alice Parker	1918	
Ice Cream	Augustus Jackson	1832	

Invention	Inventor	Date	Patent No.
Ice Cream Scooper	Alfred L. Cralle	02-02-1897	576,395
Hat Rack and Table (combined)	W.H. Ballow	03-29-1898	601,422
Ironing Board	Sarah Boone	04-26-1892	473,653
Kitchen Table	H.A. Jackson	10-06-1896	596,135
Lantern/Lamp	M.C. Harney	08-19-1884	
Lawn Sprinkler	J.W. Smith	05-04-1897	581,785
Lawnmower	J.A. Burr	05-09-1899	624,749
Lemon Squeezer	J.T. White	12-08-1896	572,849
Letter Box	George E. Becket	10-04-1892	483,525
Light Bulb Filament	Lewis Howard Latimer		
Lock	Martin Washington	07-23-1889	407,738
Method For Air Conditioning	F.M. Jones	12-07-1954	2,969,086
Method and Apparatus For Setting Thermostats	David N. Erosthwait Jr.	03-06-1928	1,661,323
Mop	Thomas W. Stewart	06-13-1893	499,402
Nursery Chair	I.O Carter	1960	
Paints & Stains	G.W. Carver		
Paper-Bag Machine	William B.	08-19-1890	434,461

Invention	Inventor	Date	Patent No.
Pastry Fork	Anna M. Mangin	03-01-1892	
Peanut Butter (along with 300 other creations from peanut butter)	G.W. Carver		
Range	Thomas Carrington	07-23-1876	180,323
Refrigerator	J. Standard	07-14-1891	455,891
Security System Utilizing Television Surveillance	Marie V. Brittan Brown	12-02-1969	3,482,037
Self Leveling Table	C.W. Allen	11-01-1898	613,436
Spring Seat For Chairs	A.P. Backburn	04-03-1888	380,420
Toilet	T. Elkins	1897	
Envelope Seal	F.W. Leslie	09-21-1897	590,325
Folding Chairs	Purdy & Sadgwar	06-11-1889	405,117
Fountain Pen	W.B. Purvis	01-07-1890	419,065
Office Machines			
Improved Vending Machine	S.H. Love	11-21-1933	1,936,515
Letter Drop Mailbox	Phillip Downing	10-27-1891	463,096
Pencil Sharpener	John L. Love	11-23-1897	597,114
Printing Press	W.A. Lavalette	09-17-1878	208,208

Invention	Inventor	Date	Patent No.
Telephone System and Apparatus	G.T. Woods	10-11-1887	371,271
Ticket Dispensing Machine	F. Jones	06-27-1939	2,163,754
Typewriting Machine	Lee Burridge	04-07-1885	315,386
Personal			
Baby Buggy	W.H. Richardson	06-18-1889	405,599
Brush	L.D. Newman	11-15-1898	614,335
Cigarette Roller	J.A. Sweeting	11-30-1897	594,501
Galoshes	A.L. Rickman	02-08-1898	598,816
Hot Comb	Walter H. Sammons	12-21-1920	1,362,823
Eye Protector	Powell Johnson	11-02-1880	234,039
Follower-Screw For Tobacco Presses , "Parker Pulverizer"	John Parker	09-02-1884	304,552
Lotions & Soaps	G.W. Carver		
Permanent Hair Wave Machine	Marjorie Joyner	11-27-1928	1,693,515
Razor Stropping Device	H. Grenon	02-18-1896	554,867

Invention	Inventor	Date	Patent No.
	Railway		
Automatic Car Coupling Device	Andrew Beard	11-23-1897	594,059
Automatic Lubrication System and Heavy Machine	Elijah McCoy	07-02-1872 1892	129,843
Cabinet Bed	Sara E. Goode	07-14-1885	322,177
Elect Railway System	G.T. Woods	11-10-1891	463,020
Elect Railway System	G.T. Woods	01-29-1902	667,110
Electric Railway System	G.T. Woods	11-19-1906	687,098
Electric Railway	W.B. Purvis	05-01-1894	519,291
Electric Railway Switch	W.B. Purvis	08-17-1897	588,176
Electric Railway Trolley	E.R. Robinson	09-19-1893	505,370
Lifesaving Guards For Street Cars	J.H. Robinson	04-25-1899	623,929
Locomotive Smoke Stack	L. Bell	05-23-1871	115,153
Rail Trestle	O.B. Claire	10-09-1888	390,753
Railway Air Brakes	Granville Woods	06-10-1902	701,981

Invention	Inventor	Date	Patent No.
Railway Signal	A.B. Blackburn	01-10-1888	376,362
Railway Switch	C.V. Richey	10-26-1897	592,448
Railway Switching Device	W.F. Burr	10-31-1899	636,197
Steam Broiler/ Radiator	Granville Woods	06-03-1884	299,894
Third Rail	Granville Woods (Subway)		
Train Alarm	R.A. Butler	06-15-1897	157,370
Trolley Car	Granville Woods	00-00-1888	
Window Ventilator For Railroad Cars	H.H. Reynolds	04-03-1883	275,271
	Sports		
Bicycle Frame	I.R. Johnson	10-10-1899	634,823
Bridle Bit	L.F. Brown	10-25-1892	484,994
Fish Hook	Henry Single	1854	
(Patented and improved.	He later sold it for $625.00)		
Golf Tee	G.F. Grant	12-12-1899	638,920
Horseshoes	Oscar E. Brown	08-23-1892	481,271
Riding Saddle	W.D. Davis	10-06-1896	568,939
Sailing Apparatus	James Forten	1850	
Self-Setting Animal Trap	W.S. Campbell	08-30-1881	246,369
Toggle Harpoon	Lewis Temple	1848	

Invention	Inventor	Date	Patent No.
Toys			
Wood Toys	Lydia Holmes	11-14-1950	2,529,692
Super Soaker	Lonnie Johnson	12-24-1991	
Weapons			
Binder System For Propellant & Explosives	Henry Sampson & Thomas & George Miley	07-07-1964	3,140,210
Case Bonding System For Cast Composite Propellant	Henry Sampson & Thomas & George Miley	10-19-1965	3,212,256
Guided Missile	Otis Boykin		
Gas Mask	Garret A. Morgan	1914	
Improvement To Military Guns	S.H. Love	04-22-1919	1,301,143
Torpedo Discharge	H. Bradberry		

* * * * *

Who Invented the Parts on the Wright Brothers' Airplane ?

Use common sense. Who invented the parts to the Wright Brothers airplane?

Wright Bros. Power flight occurred Dec. 17, 1903. However, the Propeller was invented by a Black Man, in April of 1891 Patent number 451,086. This was 12 years before the Wright Brothers flight.

The Wright Brothers received credit in the New York Public Library "SCIENCE DESK REFERENCE BOOK" as an "Achievement." There is no invention listed for them in the book relating to inventing anything on the airplane they flew.

A Black Man invented the propeller, who invented the rest of the airplane?

Who Invented the Parts That Caused the Creation of the Model T Ford ?

In 1907 the Model T Ford rolled off the assembly line, consisting of many parts, which included a motor. J. Gregory, patented a motor in April, of 1887, Patent number 361-937 (20 years before the Model T). Mr. Gregory lived in Detroit, Michigan. Was his motor modified and used?

Gasoline motors need oil to cut down friction and keep from burning up. E.J. McCoy invented an engine lubricator in May of 1873 (34 years before the Model T, Patent Number 139,407.

The "running board" was also invented by a Black man.

Who invented the parts that went on the Model T? See AUTOMOBILE above.

Note: Only one invention is listed for Henry Ford in the New York Public Library, "SCIENCE DESK REFERENCE BOOK." Henry Ford is given credit for the inventing the "conveyor belt."

Frederick M. Jones, invented the first automatic refrigeration system for long haul trucks, ships and railway. He also developed an air-conditioning unit for military field hospitals, portable x- ray machine and self-starting gasoline motor.

The above are just a few inventions credited to Blacks. There are many more that have been stolen, or they have not received credit for them.

Some United States Patents by Black Inventors

UNITED STATES PATENT OFFICE.

GRANVILLE T. WOODS, OF CINCINNATI, OHIO, ASSIGNOR TO THE WOODS ELECTRIC COMPANY.

TELEPHONE SYSTEM AND APPARATUS.

SPECIFICATION forming part of Letters Patent No. 371,241, dated October 11, 1887.

UNITED STATES PATENT OFFICE

1,936,996

TRANSMISSION AND SHIFTING MEANS THEREFOR

Richard B. Spikes, San Francisco, Calif.

Application December 17, 1932
Serial No. 647,772

8 Claims. (Cl. 74—58)

UNITED STATES PATENT OFFICE.

ELIJAH McCOY, OF YPSILANTI, MICHIGAN.

IMPROVEMENT IN LUBRICATORS FOR STEAM-ENGINES.

Specification forming part of Letters Patent No. **130,305**, dated August 6, 1872.

UNITED STATES PATENT OFFICE.

ELIJAH McCOY, OF DETROIT, MICHIGAN, ASSIGNOR TO HENRY C. HODGES AND CHARLES C. HODGES.

LUBRICATOR.

SPECIFICATION forming part of Letters Patent No. 261,166, dated July 18, 1882.

Application filed June 6, 1882. (No model.)

UNITED STATES PATENT OFFICE.

JAN E. MATZELIGER, OF LYNN, MASSACHUSETTS, ASSIGNOR, BY MESNE ASSIGNMENTS, TO THE CONSOLIDATED HAND METHOD LASTING MACHINE COMPANY, OF NASHUA, NEW HAMPSHIRE; GEORGE W. MOULTON EXECUTOR OF JAN E. MATZELIGER, DECEASED.

LASTING-MACHINE.

SPECIFICATION forming part of Letters Patent No. 459,899, dated September 29, 1891.

Application filed August 14, 1885. Serial No. 174,378. (No model.)

UNITED STATES PATENT OFFICE.

LEE S. BURRIDGE AND NEWMAN R. MARSHMAN, OF NEW YORK, N. Y.

TYPE-WRITING MACHINE.

SPECIFICATION forming part of Letters Patent No. 315,386, dated April 7, 1885.

Application filed March 22, 1884. (No model.)

Special Mention:

Paul R. Williams, Master Architect creator and designer of the restaurant and theme building of the Los Angeles International Airport.

For other achievements of Paul R. Williams in design, read:

"PAUL R. WILLIAMS ARCHITECT: A LEGACY OF STYLE"
by Karen Hudson

Chapter 12

MESSAGE TO THE WHITE RACE

You have been misled, deceived and lied to for centuries. The power structure of the world continually feeds the fuel of racism as a deterrent to keep the minds of Blacks and Whites on Civil Rights while they engage in other activities that would not be approve if you were really aware of what's going on in this country.

Now that you have been exposed to the truth, what are you going to do? Are you ready to stand up for the truth?

* * * * *

School Shooting and White Denial

by Tim Wise

"I can think of no other way to say this, so here goes: White people need to pull our heads out of our collective ass.

"Two more White children are dead and thirteen are injured, and another "nice" community is scratching its blonde head, utterly perplexed at how a school shooting the likes of the one last week in Santee, California could happen. After all, as the Mayor of the town said in an interview with CNN: We're a solid town, a good town, with good kids, a good church-going town Urban and

All-American town." Yeah, well maybe that's the problem.

"I said this after Columbine and no one listened so I'll say it again: White people live in an utter state of self-delusion. We think danger is black, brown and poor, and if we can just move far enough away from "those people" in the cities we'll be safe. If we can just find an "all-American" town, life will be better, because "things like this just don't happen here."

"This is completely without reason. In case you hadn't noticed, "here" is about the only place these kinds of things do happen. Oh, sure, there is plenty of violence in urban communities and schools. But mass murder wholesale slaughter take-a-gun-and-see-how-many-you-can-kill kinda craziness seems made for those safe places: the White suburbs or rural communities.

"And yet once again, we hear the FBI insist there is no "profile" of a school shooter. Come again? White boy after White boy after White boy, with very few exceptions to that rule (and none in the mass shooting category), decides to use their classmates for target practice, and yet there is no profile? Imagine if all these killers had been black: would we still hesitate to put a racial face on the perpetrators? Doubtful.

"Indeed, if any Black child in America - especially in the mostly White suburbs of Littleton, or Santee were to openly discuss their plans to murder fellow students, as happened both at Columbine and now Santana High, you can bet your ass that somebody would have turned them in, and the cops would have beat them to their doorstep. But when White people discuss their murderous intentions, our stereotypes of what danger looks like cause us to ignore it-they're just "talking" and won't really do anything.

"How many kids have to die before we rethink that nonsense? How many dazed and confused parents, Mayors and Sheriffs do we have to listen to, describing how "normal" and safe their community is, and how they just don't understand what went wrong?

"I'll tell you what went wrong and it's not TV, rap music, video games or lack of prayer in school. What went wrong is that White Americans decided to ignore dysfunction and violence when it only affected other communities, and thereby blinded themselves to the inevitable creeping of chaos, which never remains isolated too long. What affects the urban "ghetto" today will be coming to a Wal-Mart near you tomorrow, and unless you address the emptiness, pain, isolation and lack of hope felt by children of color and the poor, then don't be shocked when the support systems aren't there for your kids either.

"What went wrong is that we allowed ourselves to the lulled into a false sense of security by media representations of crime and violence that portray both as the province of those who are anything but White like us. We ignore the warning signs, because in our minds the warning signs don't live in our neighborhood, but across town, in that place where we lock our car doors on the rare occasion we have to drive there. That false sense of security—the result of racist and class-ist stereotypes—then gets people killed. And still we act amazed.

"But listen up my fellow White Americans: your children are no better, no nicer, no more moral, no more decent than anyone else. Dysfunction is all around you, whether you choose to recognize it or not.

"According to the Centers for Disease Control, and Department of Health and Human Services, it is your children, and not those of the urban ghetto, who are most likely to use drugs. That's right: White high school students are seven times more likely than blacks to have used cocaine, eight times more likely to have smoked crack; ten times more likely to have used LSD and seven times more likely to have used heroin. In fact, there are more White high school students who have used crystal methamphetamine (the most addictive drug on the streets) than there are black students who smoke cigarettes.

"What's more, White youth ages 12-17 are more likely to sell drugs: 34% more likely, in fact than their black counterparts. And it is White youth that are twice as likely to binge drink, and nearly twice as likely as blacks to drive drunk. And White males are twice as likely to bring weapons to school as are black males.

"And yet I would bet a valued body part that there aren't 100 White people in Santee, California, or most any other "nice" community who have ever heard a single one of the statistics above. Even though they were collected by government agencies using these folks' tax money for the purpose. Because the media doesn't report on White dysfunction.

"A few years ago, U.S. News ran a story entitled "A Shocking Look at Blacks and Crime." Yet never have they or any other new outlet discussed the "shocking" Whiteness of these shoot-em-ups. Indeed, every time media commentators discuss the similarities in these crimes they mention that the shooters were boys, they were loners, they got picked on, but never do they seem to notice a certain highly visible melanin deficiency. Color-blind, I guess.

"White-blind is more like it, as I figure these folks would spot color mighty damn quick were some of it to stroll into their community. Santee's Whiteness is so taken for granted by its residents that the Mayor, in that CNN interview, thought nothing of saying on the one had that the town was 82 percent White, but on the other hand that "this is America."

"That is not America, and especially is not California where Whites are only half of the population. This is a town that is removed from America, and yet its mayor thinks they are the normal ones-so much so that when asked about racial diversity, replied that there weren't many of different "ethni-tis-tities." Not a word. Not even close. I'd like to think that after this one, people would wake up. Take note. Rethink their stereotypes of which the dangerous ones are. But deep down, I know better. The folks hitting the snooze button on this none-too-subtle alarm are my own people, after all, and I know their blindness like the back of my hand."

By Tim Wise

Mr. Wise is a Nashville-based writer and activist and can be reached at tjwise@mindspring.com

* * * * *

"What's Wrong with Our Children ?"

Here's a question posed by a student to God:

Dear God,
Why didn't you save the school children in Littleton, Colorado ?
Sincerely,
Concerned Student

Dear Concerned Student
I am not allowed in schools.
Sincerely,
God

Now read below for how this unfolded in an incredibly short period of time:

Let's see, I think it started when Madeline Murray O'Hair complained she didn't want any prayer in our schools. And we said, OK...

Then, someone said you better not read the Bible in school, the Bible that says, "Thou shall not kill," "Thou shall not steal," and "Love your neighbor as yourself." And we said, OK...

Dr. Benjamin Spock said we shouldn't spank our children when they misbehave because their little personalities would be warped and we might damage their self-esteem. And we said, an expert should know what he's talking about so we won't spank them anymore.

Then someone said teacher and principals better not discipline our children when they misbehave. And the school administrators said no faculty member in this school better touch a student when they misbehave because we don't want any bad publicity, and we surely don't want to be sued. And we accepted their reasoning.

Then someone said, let's let our daughters have abortions if they want, and they don't even have to tell their parents. And we said, that's a grand idea...

Then some wise school board member said, since boys will be boys and they're going to do it anyway, let's give our sons all the condoms they want, so they can have all the fun they desire, and we won't have to tell their parents they got them at school. And we said, that's another great idea...

Then some of our top elected officials said it doesn't matter what we do in private as long as we do our jobs. And we said, it doesn't matter what anybody, including the President, does in private as long as we have jobs and the economy is good...

And then someone said let's print magazines with pictures of nude women and call it wholesome down-to earth appreciation for the beauty of the female body. And we said we have no problem with that.

And someone else took that appreciation a step further and published pictures of nude children and then stepped further still by making them available on the Internet. And we said, everyone's entitled to free speech...

And the entertainment industry said let's make TV shows and movies that promote profanity, violence and illicit sex. And let's record music that encourages rape, drugs, murder, suicide, and satanic themes. And we said, it's just entertainment and it has no adverse effect and nobody takes it seriously anyway, so go right ahead...

Now we're asking ourselves why our children have no conscience, why they don't know right from wrong, and why it doesn't bother them to kill strangers, classmates or even themselves.

Undoubtedly, if we thought about it long and hard enough, we could figure it out. I'm sure it has a great deal to do with...

"WE REAP WHAT WE SOW."

Received as a handout
Author Unknown
Posted in the Interest of Black People's Education

* * * * *

Chapter 13

MESSAGE TO THE BLACK RACE

For centuries we have been asked, "Why don't our race stick together, support each others businesses, etc. Perhaps Willie Lynch was the cause, but by now we should have been able to understand and push past his mentality. When you divide a people, you can always conquer them. Some Blacks have allowed themselves to go from a type of "physical slavery to a "slave mentality;" allowing others to direct our destiny. The following is the Willie Lynch letter. I hate to say that it's still working today. Let's bury Willie Lynch.

Willie Lynch was a White slave owner who advised slave owners in 1712, on methods to control their Black slaves. Lynch wrote a book called "Lets Make A Slave: The Origin and Development of a Social Being Called a Negro." Lynch's book outlined how to control and manipulate Blacks, creating mistrust and conflict among themselves. Lynch's teaching inspired slave owners to name the process of "lynching" after him.

The Willie Lynch Letter

"Gentlemen:

"I greet you here on the bank of the James River, in the year of our lord, one thousand seven hundred and twelve. First, I shall thank you, The Gentlemen of the Colony of Virginia, for bringing me here. I am here to help you solve some of your problems with slaves. Your invitation reached me on my modest plantation in the West Indies, where I have experimented with some of the newest and still oldest methods for control of slaves. Ancient Rome would envy us if my program were implemented. As our boat sailed south on the James River, named after our illustrations King, whose version of the Bible we cherish, I saw enough to know that your problem is not unique. While Rome used cords of wood as crosses for standing human bodies along its old highways in great numbers, you are here using the tree and rope on occasion.

"I caught the whiff of dead slave hanging from a tree a couple of miles back. You are not only losing valuable stock by hangings, you are having uprisings, slaves are running away, your crops are sometimes left in the fields too long for maximum profit, you suffer occasional fires, your animal are killed. Gentleman, you know what your problems are. I do not need to elaborate, I am not here to enumerate your problems, I am here to introduce you to a method of solving them.

"In my boat here, I have a fool proof method for controlling your black slaves. I guarantee every one of you that, if installed correctly, it will control the slaves for at least 300 years. My method is simple, any member of your family or any overseer can use it.

"I have outlined a number of differences among the slaves and I take these differences and make them bigger. I use fear, distrust, and envy for control purposes. These methods have worked on my modest plantation in the West Indies, and it will work throughout the South. Take this simple little list of differences, and think about them. On top of my list is "Age," but it is there only because it starts with and "A;" the second is "Color," or shade; there is intelligence, size, sex, size of plantation, attitudes of owners, whether the slaves live in the valley, on a hill, East, West, North, South have fine or course hair, or is tall or short. Now that you have a list of differences, I shall assure you that distrust is stronger then trust, and envy is stronger than adulation, respect or admiration.

"The black slave after receiving this indoctrination, shall carry on and will become self re-fueling and self generating for hundreds of years, maybe thousands.

"Don't forget, you must pit the old black verses the young black male, and the young black male against the old black male. You must use the dark skin slaves versus the light skin slaves and the light skin slaves verses the dark skin slaves. You must use the female verses the male, and the male verses the female. You must also have your White servants and overseers distrust all black, but it is necessary that you slaves trust and depend on us. They must love, respect and trust only us.

"Gentlemen, these kits are your keys to control, use them. Have your wives and children use them, never miss an opportunity. My plan is guaranteed, and the good thing about this plan is

> that, if used intensely for one year, the slaves themselves will remain perpetually distrustful."
>
> Thank you, Gentlemen
> Willie Lynch, 1712

* * * * *

We have allowed ourselves to be pitted against one another for decades, always doing anything, to be accepted by members of other races. At the same time, many other races only get involved with us when they can get something from us. They set up shops and stores in our area, make money from us and take it into the area where they live.

Have you ever stopped to think, "Our children are brought up, in most cases, handing their money to people of other races?" After years of this practice, they think this is the way it should be.

For all these years, the White man has taught us to dislike each other; for one reason or another. There has been and still is a plan to eliminate us or divide us in such a manner where, as a race we will be ineffective.

Many gains Blacks have made have been due to the mistakes of Whites. For instance, we have had Black mayors in several large cities such as Los Angeles, Chicago, Detroit, Atlanta, New York, etc. What was the White mistake? The "White flight," when the White people moved from the inner cities, they left the voting power to the Blacks and other minorities.

Now many Whites realize what they have done, they are moving back to the cities. Can you imagine what will happen? For the first time in 20 years, Los Angeles does not have a Black mayor.

As a race of people we refuse to face the fact that the power structure is out to eliminate the Black race. AIDS was developed to depopulate Africa. It's working, some nations in Africa have over 50% of the population with AIDS.

Over 25% of the Black males from the age of 18 to 25 years are either in jail or dead.

* * * * *

People in power will do anything to maintain that power. Read the below article. Since the government was in control of everything, no records can be found of the numbers of Black People slaughtered. However, due to the nature of apartheid, we know over the years millions were slaughtered. There were times when whole villages were slaughtered. READ THE FOLLOWING. This is the mentality of the people that had control over a country of Black People. A few White people invaded a country of peaceful Black People, terrorized and slaughtered millions.

Plus: Mass Genocide Planned In South Africa? Read Botha's Sinister Plan Page 15

Challenger

WE WISH TO PLEAD OUR OWN CAUSE. TOO LONG HAVE OTHERS SPOKEN FOR US

BUFFALO, NEW YORK

MASS GENOCIDE PLANNED?
BOTHA'S SINISTER PLAN AGAINST AFRICANS REVEALED
November 5, 1986, Page 15

"(Ed. Notes

"Following are excerpts from a speech by past South African President P.W. Botha to his cabinet last year. The speech in it's entirety appeared in the August 18,1985 edition of the Sunday Times, a South African newspaper and was written by David G. Millu. The language and contents of Botha's speech is shocking. We're publishing it to expose the sick and dangerous mentality at the helm of that country. Why is apartheid so evil and hatred? Read on. Special thanks to Charles Montgomery (Kenya Nkrumab) of Attica for this information)."

Speech by South Africa's Past President Botha

"My Beloved White Afrikaaners,

"Greetings to all of you brothers and sisters in the name of our holy blood. On behalf of our precious country and myself, Botha, the president of the Republic of South Africa, I take this opportunity to thank and congratulate you barely for your courage and determination in giving me your strong hand to keep the Afrikaaner flag flying high. We are going through trying time, and have chosen to write to you to assure you of my dedication and solidarity with you through fire and brimstone. We live among greedy savages who are after our blood, who hate us and want to take from us what we have acquired. But do not forget we are gifted and united people. Long live the White Afrikaaner flag! Long Live Afrikaanerdom!

"Do not see me as mere Botha by name, but the very living spirit and promise of your White brothers and sisters. Verily I say unto you, this is our God-given land for which we should fight to the very last drop of blood. We cannot simply stand and watch all the laurels we have created being plundered by these barbaric and lazy killers. Pretoria has been made by the White mind for the White man. We are not obliged even in the least to try to prove to anybody and to the Blacks that we are superior people. We have demonstrated that to the Blacks in a thousand and one ways. The republic of South Africa that we know of today has not been created by wishful thinking. We have created it at the expense of intelligence, sweat and blood.

"The blood of our forefathers was poured on this very land for our salvation. We have therefore, a great responsibility to safeguard our treasure, our history and pride. He cannot be wrong, who fights for his own survival and right. Beloved citizens, you are aware of the kind of nonsense being spread all over the world about us. We have been labeled everything bad; but this is not because we are worse than anybody else. Come to think of it my honorable citizens: The racism they talk about didn't begin with the White Afrikaaner. It has always been a fact of this life.

"I am simply trying to prove to you all that there is nothing unusual we are doing that the so-called civilized world are not doing. We are simply an honest people who have come out aloud with a clear philosophy of how we want to live our own White life. We do not pretend like other Whites that we like Blacks. The fact that Blacks look like human beings does not necessarily make them sensible human beings. Hedgehogs are not porcupines and lizards are not crocodiles simply because they look alike. If God wanted us to be equal to the Blacks, he would have created us all of uniform color and intellect.

"But he created us differently Whites, Blacks, Yellow. Rulers and the ruled. Intellectually, we are superior to the Blacks; that has been proven beyond any reasonable doubt over years. I believe that the African is an honest, God-fearing person, who has demonstrated practically the right way of being. He does not engage in hypocrisy of all these others who love sounding substantive of political hot air or to make the world believe that they are better off *(illegible)* is more concerned about human welfare than we are. We give Blacks employment and a thousand and one other amenities."

"MY SCIENTISTS HAVE COME UP
WITH A DRUG THAT CAN BE
SMUGGLED INTO THEIR BREWS
TO EFFECT SLOW POISONING
RESULTS AND FERTILITY
DESTRUCTION."

"Nevertheless, it is comforting to known that behind the scenes, Europe, America, Canada, Australia and all the others are behind us in spite of what they say. For diplomatic relations, we all know what language should be used and where. To prove my point comrades, does anyone of you know a White country without an investment or interest in South Africa? Who buys our diamonds? Who buys our gold? Who is helping us develop the nuclear weapon? The very truth is that we are their people and they are our people. It's a big secret. The strength of our economy is backed by America, Britain, Germany, and I have on my list a number of Black countries - no kidding. Comrade Afrikaaners, survival for the fittest didn't begin with us. It is not the design of the chicken that it be eaten by the hawk. It is in nature's that the hawk should eat the chicken, but aren't they both birds? It is nature's way that small fish should be eaten by the big fish. It is our strong conviction therefore that the Black is the raw material for the White man.

"WORKING THROUGH DRINKS AND MANUFACTURING OF SOFT DRINKS GEARED TO THE BLACKS COULD PROMOTE THE CHANNELS OF REDUCING THEIR POPULATION."

"So brothers and sisters, let us join hands together to fight against this black devil. I appeal to all Afrikaaners to come out with any creative means of fighting this war. Surely God cannot forsake his own people whom we are. By now every one of us has seen it practically that Blacks cannot rule themselves. Give them guns and they will kill each other. They are good in nothing else but making noise, dancing, marrying many wives and including in sex. You have just to look around and take a look of what their independent countries have achieved. Don't we know what is happening in Ghana, Mozambique, Sudan,

Nigeria, Uganda, Egypt, to name but a few. Nothing else but chaos, bloodshed, corruption and starvation such as in Ethiopia. Let us all accept that the Black man is the symbol of poverty, mental inferiority, (illegible) and emotional impotence. Isn't it possible therefore that the White man is created to rule the Black man?"

"OUR EXPERTS WORK DAY AND
NIGHT TO SET THE BLACK MAN
AGAINST HIS FELLOW MAN.
HIS INFERIOR SENSE OF MORALS
CAN BE EXPLOITED BEAUTIFULLY."

"The food supply channel should be used. We have developed excellent slow killing poisons and fertility destroyers. Our only fear is in case such stuff get into their hands as they are bound to start using it against you. Think of the many Blacks working for us in our domestic quarters. However, we are doing the best we can to make sure that the stuff remains strictly in our hands. Secondly, most Blacks are vulnerable to money inducements. I have set aside a special fund to exploit this venue. The old trick of divide and rule is still very valid today. Our experts should work day and night to set the Black man against his fellow man. His inferior sense of morals can be exploited beautifully. And here is a creature that lacks forethought. There is need for us to combat him in long-term projections that he cannot suspect. The average Black does not plan his life beyond a year: that stance, for example, should be exploited. My special department is already working round the clock to come out with a long-term operation blueprint.

"I am also sending a special request to all Afrikaaner mothers to double their birth rate. It may be necessary too to set up a population boom industry by putting up centers where we employ and support fully White young men and women to produce children for the nation. We are also investigating the merit of uterus rentals as a possible means of seeding up growth of our population through surrogate mothers. For the time being, we should also engage a higher gear to make sure that Black men are separated from their women and fines be imposed upon married wives who bear illegitimate children. I have a committee working on finding better methods of inciting Blacks against each other and encouraging murders among themselves. Murder cases among Blacks should bear very little punishment in order to encourage them. My scientists have come up with a drug that could be smuggled into their brews to effect slow poisoning results and fertility destruction. Working through drinks and manufacturing of soft drinks geared to the Blacks could promote the channels of reducing their population.

"Our combat unity is now training special White girls in the use of slow poisoning drugs. Ours is not a war that we can use the atomic bomb to destroy the Blacks, so we must use our intelligence to effect this. The person-to-person encounter can be very effective. As the records show that the Black man is dying to go to bed with the White women, here is our unique opportunity. Our sex Mercenary Squad should go out and camouflage with Apartheid Fighters while doing their operations quietly, administering slow-killing poison and fertility destroyers to those Blacks they thus befriend. We are modifying the Sex Mercenary Squad by introducing White Men who should go for the militant Black woman and any other vulnerable Black women. We have received a new supply of prostitutes from Europe and America who are desperate and too keen to take up the appointments. Money can do anything for you. So while we have it, we should make best use of it.

"In the meantime, my beloved White citizens, do not take to heart, what the world says, and don't be ashamed of being called racists. I don't mind being called the architect and King of Apartheid. I shall not become a monkey simply because someone calls me a monkey. I will still remain your bright star. His Excellency Botha. My last appeal is that the maternity hospital operations should be intensified. We are not paying those people to help bring Black babies to this world but to eliminate them on the very delivery moment. If this department worked very efficiently, a great deal could be achieved. My government has set aside a special fund for erecting more hospital and clinics to promote this program."

P.W. Botha
Past President of South Africa

* * * * *

The above statement from Botha truly shows his intent and mentality. However, there are many other White people that share his views.

* * * * *

Why Can't You Get It? "Are You Stupid?"

> "No matter what we do to you,
> you make us rich by
> spending your money with us."

Dear Black Americans:

After all of these years and all we have been through together, we think it's appropriate for us to show our gratitude for all you have done for us. We have chastised you, criticized you, punished you, and in some cases even apologized to you, but we have never formally, nor publicly, thanked you for your never-ending allegiance and support to our cause. Cause we want your money; that's all.

This is our open letter of thanks to a unique people, a forgiving people, a steadfast people, and a brave people: BLACK AMERICANS. We will always be in debt to you for your labor. You built this country and were responsible for the great wealth we still enjoy today. Upon your backs, laden with stripes we sometimes had to apply for disciplinary reasons, you carried our nation. We thank you for that. We thank you for your diligence and tenacity. Even when we refused to allow you to even walk in our shadow, you followed close behind believing that some day we would come to accept you and treat you like men and women. Your strength in the face of adversity cannot be understated. You are truly a great people, and we thank you so much!

We publicly acknowledge Black People for raising our children, attending to our sick and preparing our meals while we were occupied with the trappings of the good life. Even during the times when we found pleasure in your women and enjoyed seeing one of your men lynched, maimed and burned, some of you continued to watch over us and our belongings. We simply cannot thank you enough. Your bravery on the battlefield, despite being classified as three-fifths of a man, was and still is, outstanding and beyond the call of duty. We often watched in awe as you went about your prescribed chores and assignments, sometimes laboring in the hot sun for 12 hours, to assist us realizing our dreams of wealth and good fortune. You were always there, and we thank you.

No that we control at least 90% of all the resources and wealth of this nation, we have Black People to thank the most. You were there when it all began, and you are still with us today, protecting us from those Black People who have the temerity to speak out against our past transgressions. How can we thank your for your dedication? You warned us about Denmark Vessey. You let us know about Gabriel Posser's plans; and you called our attention to Nat Turner. And, you even sounded the alarm when old John Brown came calling Harper's Ferry. Some of you still warn us today. Thank you, thank you, thank you!

Now, as we look out upon our enormous wealth, and as we assess our tremendous control of the resources of this country, we can only think of the sacrifices you and your families made to make all of this possible. You are indeed fantastic, and we will forever be in your debt. To think of how you have looked out for us for hundreds of years and to see you still doing the same thing today is simply amazing!

Thank you for continuing to bring 95% of what you earn to our businesses. That is so gracious of you! Thanks for buying our Hilfigers, Mercedes, Nikes and all the other brands you so adore. Your purchase of these products really makes us feel that we are at least giving something back to you for your patronage. After all, in the past the brands we put on you were quite painful, but those of today can be worn proudly because they give you a sense of self-esteem, right? But it's the least we can do for a people who have treated us so well.

Your super-rich athletes, entertainers, intellectual, and businesspersons (both legal and illegal) exchange most of their money for our cars, jewelry, homes, and clothing. What a windfall they have provided for us. The less fortunate among you spend all they have at our neighborhood stores enabling us to open even more stores. Sure you complain about us, but you never do anything to hurt us economically! You are a very special people. Thank you.

Oh yes, allow us to think you for not bogging yourselves down with business of doing business with your own people. We can take care of that for you. Please don't trouble yourselves with it. Yes, you were very successful at it after slavery ended and even as recently as 1960, but you know what happened when you began to build your own communities and do business with one another. Some of the "lower ones" of our kind burned you out – time and time again. So why bother? In today's business environment your own people will not support you anyway.

You just keep doing business with us. It's safer that way. Besides, everything you need we make anyway, even Kente' cloth. You just continue to dance, sing, fight, get high, go to prison, backbite, envy, mistrust and hate one another. Have yourselves a good time, and we'll take care of you. It's the least we can do, considering all you've done for us. Heck you deserve it, Black People.

For your labor which created our wealth, for your resisting the message of trouble-making Blacks like Washington, Daleany, Garvey, Bethune, Tubman, and Truth and for fighting and dying on our battlefields, we thank you. For allowing us to move into your neighborhood, we will forever be grateful to you. For your unceasing desire to be near us and for hardly ever following through on your threats due to your lack of reciprocity and equity – we than you so much.

We also appreciate your acquiescence to our political agendas, abdicating your own economic self-sufficiency, and for working so diligently for the economic well-being of our people. Your are real troopers. And even though the 13th, 14th, and 15th Amendments were written for you and many of your relatives died for the rights described therein, you did not resist when we changed those Black rights to Civil Rights and allowed virtually every other group to take advantage of them as well. Black People, you are something else! Your dependence upon us to do the right thing irrespective of what we do to you and the many promises we have made and broken, is beyond our imagination! But, this time we will make it right, we promise. Trust us!

Tell you what. You don't need your own hotels. You can continue to stay in ours. You have no need for supermarkets when you can shop at ours 24 hours a day. Why should you even think about owning banks? You have plenty now. And don't waste your energies trying to break into manufacturing. You've worked hard enough in our fields. Relax, have a party. We'll sell you everything. And when you die, we'll even bury you at a discount. Now how's that for gratitude?

Finally, the best part. You went beyond the pale and turned your children over to us for their education. With what we have taught them, it's likely they will continue in a mode similar to the one you have followed for the past 45 years. When Mr. Lynch walked the banks of the James River in 1712 and said he would make "your kind" a slave for 300 years, little did we realize the truth of his prediction. Just 13 more years and his promise will come to fruition. But, with two generations of your children having gone through our education system, we look forward to at least another 50 years of prosperity. Wow! Things could not be better – and it's all because of you. For all you have done, we thank you from the bottom of our hearts, Black Americans. You're the best friend any group of people could ever have!

Sincerely,
All Other Americans

WHAT HAPPENS NEXT IS UP TO YOU!

Received as a Handout
Author Unknown
Posted in the Interest of Black People's Education

* * * * *

One day a conversation was overheard between two Orientals. One man told the other, "Blacks will buy anything, but don't try to own anything. If you leave them alone, they will self destruct."

SLAVERY

**THE 13TH AMENDMENT OF THE CONSTITUTION
BROKE THE PHYSICAL CHAINS OF SLAVERY.
LET KNOWLEDGE OVERCOME
SLAVE MENTALITY."**
By Dr. Romeo L. Taylor, Sr.

New Attitude

Malcolm X said,

"THE GREATEST MISTAKE OF THE MOVEMENT HAS BEEN TRYING TO ORGANIZEA SLEEPING PEOPLE AROUND SPECIFIC GOALS.

YOU HAVE TO WAKE THE PEOPLE UP FIRST, THEN YOU'LL GET RESULTS."

* * * * *

"THIS SHOULD BE YOUR WAKE UP CALL!"

Chapter 14

WHAT MANY WHITES THINK ABOUT BLACKS !

Blacks Don't Read

They are still our slaves. We can continue to reap profits from the Blacks without the effort of physical slavery. Look at the current methods of containment that they use on themselves:

Ignorance, Greed, and Selfishness

Their IGNORANCE is the primary weapon of containment. A great man once said, "The best way to hide something from Black People is to put it in a book." We live now in the Information Age. They have gained the opportunity to read any book on any subject through the efforts of their fight for freedom, yet they refuse to read. There are numerous books available at Borders, Barnes & Noble, and Amazon.com, not to mention their own Black Bookstores that provide solid blueprints to reach economic equality (which should have been their fight all along), but few read consistently, if at all.

GREED is another powerful weapon of containment. Blacks, since the abolition of slavery, have had large amounts of money at their disposal. Last year they spent 10 billion dollars during Christmas, out of their 450 billion dollars in total yearly income (2.22%). Any of us can use them as our target market, for any business venture we care to dream up, no matter how outlandish, they will buy into it. Being primarily a consumer people, they function totally by greed. They continually want more, with little thought of saving or investing. They would rather buy some new sneaker than invest in starting a business. Some even neglect their children to have the latest Tommy or Fubu. They still believe that having a Mercedes, and a big house gives them "status" or that they have achieved the American Dream. They are fools! The vast majority of their people are still in poverty because their greed holds them back for collectively making better communities. With the help of BET (Black Entertainment Television), and the rest of their Black media that often broadcast destructive images into their own homes, we will continue to see huge profits like those of Tommy and Nike. (Tommy Hilfiger has jeered them, saying he doesn't want their money, and look at how the fools spend more with him than ever before!). They'll continue to show off to each other while we build solid communities with the profits from our businesses that we market to them.

SELFISHNESS, ingrained in their minds through slavery, is one of the major ways we can continue to contain them. One of their own, Dubois said that there was an innate division in their culture. A "Talented Tenth" he called it. He was correct in his deduction that there are segments of their culture that has achieved some "form" of success. However, that segment missed the fullness of his work. They didn't read that the "Talented Tenth" was then responsible to aid the "Non-Talented Ninety Percent" in achieving a better life. Instead, that segment has created another class, a Buppie

(Black Yuppie) class that looks down on their people or aids them in a condescending manner. They will never achieve what we have. Their selfishness does not allow them to be able to work together on any project or endeavor of substance. When they do together, their selfishness lets their egos get in the way of the goal. Their so-called help organizations seem to only want to promote their name without making any real change in their community. They are content to sit in conferences and conventions in our hotels, and talk about what they will do, while they award plaques to the best speakers, not the best doers. Is there no end to their selfishness? They steadfastly refuse to see that TOGETHER EACH ACHIEVES MORE (TEAM)! They do not understand that they are no better than each other because of what they own. In fact, most of those Buppies are but one or two paychecks away from poverty. All of which is under control of our pens in our offices and our bedrooms. Yes, we will continue to contain them as long as they refuse to read, continue to buy anything they want, and keep thinking they are "helping" their communities by paying dues to organizations which do little other than hold lavish conventions in our hotels. By the way, don't worry about any of them reading this letter, remember, "THEY DON'T READ!!!!"

Received as a handout
Author Unknown
Posted in the Interest of Black People's Education

* * * * *

Received and Reviewed from the
Afrocentric News Network

Through an exhaustive investigation, we have uncovered quips, quotes, and hand written notes of a Fifth Column and Totalitarian in this country. You may, if you like, call them as we do, the "Disciples of Willie Lynch." Here are scant morsels of the Fifth Column's scathing critique of Black leadership in America.

From the "Disciples of Willie Lynch"

"To Black Leaders,

"Through print and press-conferences, radio and television mediums alike, you have provided us startling evidence that we have absolutely nothing to worry about.

"You remain prisoners of your own folly, psychological weaknesses, lack of vision and commitment. More importantly, we have not one scintilla of interest in solving your Rubik's-Cube type problems. In fact, let's examine your dreams and murder them with a gang of facts.

"You people dream of political power. However, the Republican and Democratic parties are wings of the same bird, and cauldrons for legalized racketeering. Consequently, the election process is a sneak preview of stolen merchandise, after which, you get the best politicians that money can buy.

"Yet, you people continue as the chief apologist for the Democratic Party. Nikolai Lenin once said: "People always have been and they always will be ...'useful fools'... and stupid victims of deceit and self-deception in politics." He was right.

"You people say education is the key, and we agree. In fact, children are the most curious beings on earth. Yet, go into a classroom and observe the mindless looks on the faces of your children-are their eyes flushed with enthusiasm? No! Most of them are either irritable, listless, or bored out of their minds.

"Where has their sense of curiosity or wonderment gone? Who wrestled it away from them? Who's emasculating the genius in your children? How do your children develop a fear of subjects like math and science? How does any credible educator or institute of learning, fail to arouse in your children: a love of business, economics, literature, history, etc? Here's a hint.
Everyday those marvelous little souls are herded into classrooms like sheep. Once inside of our psychological torture chambers, their zeal to discover and learn are summarily cremated. You may thank our hand-picked behavioral psychiatrist, social engineers and change-agents, for infecting your children with degrees of intellectual inferiority, anxiety, and acute mental sterility.

"Meanwhile, you people are as exercised about this matter as a mummy in a mausoleum.

"More importantly, we have successfully turned

college campuses in incubators and center for cognitive dissonance and thought-control. Translation? You people are not educated, but indoctrinated, and thus you shall remain in our opinion, convincingly so. Perhaps in case of you people it's true: that until one exhaust ignorance and habit, intelligence dare not appear.

"You people dream of economic power and we understand your quest. In fact, your ancestors were formidable business merchants and extraordinary commodity trader. But now all you people trade are mostly stories on sports, entertainment, racism and gossip.

"Saving money and investing are signs of a highly intelligent and industrious people. But since you save little or nothing, you own little or nothing. Consumer debt and bankruptcy filings amongst you people are at or near record highs. Still, you beg us to issue you credit and take you into bondage—again!

"Witness the dilapidated building, run down schools, and tattered homes (with bars) where you frequent. Indeed, the disintegration of your neighborhoods and cities are squarely before everyone's eyes. And no one with a choice dares to live amongst you.

"Ever mindful of these facts, oily politicians' demand a myriad of economic inferno programs like aid packages, empowerment zones, employment shams, and credit schemes to pacify you. But isn't it interesting that while poverty is a multibillion dollar industry, somehow (wink-

wink), you people continue to suffocate in its muck and mire?

"African use to build nations and systems-now you merely get worked by the system. Your forefathers left you a legacy of intellectual genius, economic prowess, and amazing creativity upon which to build. Accept by choice, you dishonor their memory. In fact, you people are more likely to be criminal defendants.

"And maybe we shouldn't say this: but why not make investments in strategic planning, superior management teams, knowledge, technical know-how, and your own private investment banks? After all, you folks brag about spending $500 billion a year.

"And finally, to strong people who act weak, more amusing than your whining about how we stole your culture, heritage, and legacy: is as intelligent and creative people, you can't figure out how to steal it back.

"Seriously, maybe the only thing we actually stole from you people, is your common sense.

"Until your so-called "Black Leaders" take education and economics, as seriously as you do entertainment and athletics...we'll see you on the bottom. Because surely, your apathy and disorganization, are certain, to keep you there.

"Note: As Black Leaders you will fail to analyze this message and take positive action to save your people; which by the way, requires real thinking, vision, and action. Instead, you will express your outrage, call us racist (a sure sign of an exhausted mind) and drown yourselves in fit of anger. After which, you shall lie there panting like dogs on a curb after a car chase. Why? Because it's the path of least resistance, and far easier than real organization, planning, and action."

From The "Disciples of Willie Lynch"

For more information go to:
www.afrocentricnews.com/html/hart_willie_lynch_400

* * * * *

Cultural Conflict . . . "They Say We Are Mad"

Speech given in London, relating to the attitude of the government and many Brits concerning Blacks in England.

Given by Clarence C. Thompson, General Secretary West Indian Standing Conference, in mid-1990.

"Ladies and Gentlemen,

"On behalf of the Standing Conference of West Indian Organization I wish to thank the Health Education Authority, for giving me the opportunity to discuss the wider social issues which have demonstratively impacted upon the lives of black people, and to refute the assumptions White psychiatrists make on the sanity of Black People. There are two main schools of White thought on the sanity of people of the African Diaspora. One school argues that we are mentally deficient and that deficiency is genetic. The other argues that we cannot cope with the rigours of modern urbanization. I say to you that the labels of "genetic madness or socially depressive madness" that are heaped upon us, are the consequence of a cultural conflict, borne out of the hatred and the contempt the White races of Europe have been inflicting on the peoples of African for the past 493 years.

"Denying Africans their humanity has been the path taken to justify the holocaust of slavery, and the continuing demise is in our view, calculated to ensure that the White race can persist in the humiliation and domination of the African peoples.

"I intend to show that the power barons of today, who design laws are imbued with the same degree of inherent racism, which sanctified the holocaust of slavery. And the power barons persist in the theology of the sadism of racism because they are not sufficiently mature to be objective about the issue of race. We conclude therefore, that in instances where the consequences of the racism is a denial of human dignity or the death of a mortal, then those who framed the laws that perpetrated the sadism, cannot like Pontius Pilate wash their hands and say, "This washing absolves us from blame." Similarly, when the sick die because of the deliberate cuts in the resources to which they are entitled, then those who took the decision to cut resources are culpable; and in a mature society, would be and should be charged with secondary degree murder.

"In Britain the labeling of schizophrenia is part of the syndrome of racism which:

"denied us employment comparable to educational qualifications:

"subjected our children to schools for the educationally subnormal;

"denied us access to decent housing;

"denied us access to finance for starting businesses;

"encouraged and gave legitimacy to police harassment;

"imposed much longer prison sentences for the similar crimes committed by Whites

"imposed the 1981 British Nationality necessitated Black People having to buy a nationality which was legitimately theirs.

"In our experience, it is customary to find that when a black person dies as a result of maltreatment, especially at the hands of the police, the unlawful killing is not seen as being worthy of demanding accountability – either through prosecution or discipline.

"I intend to call upon White psychiatrists to redress their dis-service to Black People. They should pause for a moment and assess the impact of their racism on their readiness to denounce Black People as mad and to use them as medical guinea pigs. They must acknowledge that their deliberate misdiagnoses are particularly responsible for the over-representation of Africans in mental institutions and prisons.

"It is essential for them to review their position. White psychiatrists tend to ignore alternative therapy, and in preference chose the needle and drugs as the best and only option. I am suggesting that you who have the power of demigods, in this branch of medicine, which is too reliant on opinion, rather that on fact, should, as a consequence take a preventive stance rather than dabble. Although I am not a psychiatrist, I am aware that many mental problems can be resolved by giving the patient a shoulder to cry on. Some tea and sympathy can be a sound catalyst for encouraging potential patients to resolve the offending problems. I have developed the "touch therapy," combined with relaxation for the management of stress. You have the option to share in a demonstration of both the method and the complementing attitude which compound into a sound alternative therapy.

Modern Consequences of Racism

"Today's psychiatrists tell us that, "We are mad and violent." But may I remind you, that before the advent of psychiatry, we had the philosophers, capitalist with their priests, bishops and popes, telling us that we were not humans and that God created to be slaves; and that

Europe had the divine right to enslave us. I say to you, that the judgements that are made on us today, are part of the same Christic sadism which reined terror on us for the last 493 years.

"Today, the part played by White psychiatrists who ignore the notion of justice and fair play in the continuing cultural conflict is central to the demise of the African peoples to: the slave-class in the British society, for as long as the two races have to co-exist; an over-representation in the mental institutions and prisons; the constant pursuit of justice which saps innovative zest, a psychological conditioning which encourages under-achievement in preference to the quest for excellence in education.

"And when against enormous odds, excellence is achieved, covert and overt racism become the barriers to accessing jobs comparative to the educational qualification; the application of overt and covert discrimination to deny access to finance for entrepreneurial pursuits; a multiplicity of deaths in police care, and for which no police officer has been held to be accountable, especially when we are told that all officers are trained in first aid; a position in which Sir Peter Imbert, London Metropolitan Police Commissioner, instead of addressing the real causes of those deaths, is seeking to have death in police custody redefined a level of injustice and lack of concern for the deaths in police custody by the Director of Public Prosecutions who in defense of the police no accountability indicates that, there is no case to answer, even though the Met has paid well over £1M in compensation;

"As consequence, no police office has been disciplined, even though in some cases there have been evidence of severe police brutality, resulting in death. We view his protective stance as cognizant of an agreement to the expendability of Black People;

"I have been bold in raising the issue. As a consequence, there are those who would say that I have a chip on my shoulder. Well I have a surprise. It's not a chip, but a log. It's a log, because as General Secretary to the Standing Conference of West Indian Organization, I am charged with the responsibility for addressing all the social needs including the quest for justice for the community. It's a log, because when Black People die in police custody, I am charged with the responsibility of trying to find out why they had to die. We at West Indian Standing Conference are then confronted with the closing of the ranks by various government institutions; all acting in concert to obscure the causes of death, by indicating that the victims, and only the victims, who played the central role in causing their own deaths.

Institutional Conspiracy in Defence of the Police

"Racism also impacts upon the decision coroners make about the cause of death, especially when Black People die while in the "care" of the police. The coroners indicate the victims, healthy young people with a zest for life, are always responsible for their own deaths. The cause of death is always one of the following – "death by misadventure, accidental death, or suicide." That kind of institutional conspiracy which is reminiscent of South Africa is now a way of life in Britain. We view this acting in concert as complicity, which is further, reinforced by police investigating police. The option for corruption is very opportune, since in this democracy, they are note required to be accountable.

"To create a semblance of independent investigation, we are given a mirage called the Police Complaints Authority, whose judgments or findings to date are not worthy of any merit. The main flaw is that it has no authority to effect justice.

The Benefits of Understanding Our Experience

"There are healthy benefits, not only for those Whites who are deemed to be as expendable as Africans, but essentially for the decision makers. We have a responsibility to teach them how to be humane. If they have souls that can be touched, then we must touch them.

"To begin the process let us focus on the evil that is inherent in the fashionable term "racism" and assess the pain and poverty it has caused, and it continues to cause amongst poor blacks in the inner cities. Let us examine my definition of "pain and poverty in the inner cities?"

"Pain is the psychological impact of racism, and poverty is the resulting deprivation that plagues the physical and social fabric of our community. I chose the inner cities because we owe a debt of gratitude of Prince Charles for recognizing that the riots of 1981 and 1985 indicated that here are major problems in the relationships between the classes. It is our view that his work triggered the Prime Minister's change in her attitude towards the poor and caused her to acknowledge that the inner cities are in crisis.

"It has to be noted, too, that we are approaching the 21st Century, and yet, there is evidence to support the view under Margaret Thatcher's Prime Ministership that society in Britain – is not sufficiently mature, to come to terms with the issue of race. She made her view public in 1979 when she said, "Britain is being swamped by an alien culture, and we must therefore end that swamping." The same applies to the United States of America, which the UK tries to emulate. They were so immature, they elected to shoot President John Kennedy, Secretary of State – Robert Kennedy, and Martin Luther King for attempting to address the issue of race.

"The pain we are made to endure is not only caused through the way we are treated in Britain, but through our common history of slavery with Africa's people in the Americas and Africa. As a consequence, we remain very alert to and hopeful when Britain criticizes Russia on Human Rights, and then we are forced to recoil in despair when Britain, because of self interest, defends and vetoes the many attempts by the United Nations to bring South Africa to heel on the very question of Human Rights. The conclusion we draw from this dichotomy is that Africa's people must remain as expendable as we were during the holocaust of slavery.

The Mental Health Argument

"The thrust of my debate will focus on racism, racial discrimination, and the ethic of class superiority to illustrate how they impact upon the mental health and the physical and social deprivation of the black community. We have identified racism as the key factor which causes and empowers police officers, who are not trained in psychiatry, to use Section 136 of the Mental Health Act, to remove any person they judge to be suffering from a mental disorder to "a place of safety" for a minimum observation period of 72 hours.

"It is also reported that under Section 86 of the Mental Health Act, Africans in psychiatric detention are being repatriated to their countries of birth. As a consequence, we call into question, both the sanity and intention of those who proposed these sections of the Act. We argue that both Section 86 and Section 136 legitimize discrimination against Black People. There are sound reasons for the conclusion the Section 136 is an extension of the activity, in which teachers were empowered with the legitimacy to place a high percentage of our children in schools for the educationally subnormal.

"It is ironic that at a Mind Conference held March 1989, a senior officer representing the Met, stated that he was concerned about the over-representation of Black People in mental institutions. He explained that he was not sure how the over representations came about, but he was sure that the police were not at fault. When asked who made the decision to take the person to a place of safety, he agreed that it was the police, but blamed the public for having called them to the scene. When asked if any of the officers making decisions on the case were trained in psychiatry, he retorted that police officers did not need training, they relied on their common sense. In hindsight, training might cause the numbers incarcerated to increase ten-fold.

"We the victims, understand how difficult it is for White teachers or police who are ordained superior, and who have been breast fed on the theology of racism, to be bestowed with the responsibility for interpreting the behavior and making objective judgments on the people they view as their inferior. It is evident that there is a cultural conflict – a conflict which sets a dangerous precedence for decisions of such sensitivity to be dependent on how one race perceives the other.

Supporting Evidence

"The evidence at Tooting Bee, London, confirmed that unlike the White patient population, twice the number of black patients were detained under Section 136. Ray Rowden, the manager of Tooting Bee confirmed that our criticisms are well founded. In an area with a 14% black population, 50% of the mental patients are young African males. Rowden, who is White, states with resounding clarity, "I believe that it comes back to the crunch of racism. If you are a young black male, there will be the subconscious perception that you are more mad and more violent. Hence the higher levels of medication and the reason for seven times more black patients being diagnosed as schizophrenic."

In an article, "Mental Health and the Black Community," Ade Coker, puts the same. He cites the fact, 'In Barnsley Hall, a large psychiatric hospital in Birmingham 50% of the patient population are black. The most common diagnosis for Black People suffering from acute stress is schizophrenia. Another major concern is the misuse of drugs in the treatment of many young black men who are seen as "threatening and dangerous.'

"The African communities do not only question the practices and assumptions made by White psychiatrist, they claim that there is sufficient evidence to support the conclusion, that Africans are being declared schizoid, so that they can be used as guinea pigs for testing a variety of drugs. There is substance in this view, since black detainees are more likely to be forcible treated, held in locked wards of secure units; and their treatment to be more reliant on drugs than on meaningful psychotherapy.

"I argue that psychiatrist, police, teachers, and those with the power and authority for writing and adjudicating the law have a responsibility to display mature moral fortitude by desisting in the use of racism as a premise for judgment. Since the Papal Bill by Pope Alexander VI in 1493, racism against Black People has resulted in the holocaust of slavery which surpasses any tragedy any other race has suffered at the hands of Christian Europeans. The time has come for you to grow in stature, and show that you are sufficiently mature to appreciate the wealth of cultures – especially the culture of Black People on God's Earth."

By Clarence C. Thompson
General Secretary
West Indian Standing Conference
London, England

* * * * *

Chapter 15

IT'S NEVER TOO LATE

The Turtle and the Fox

One day a fox was bragging how fast he was and he could out run all the other animals. There was a lion there that had the personality of Don King. He was a promoter so he bet the fox and other animals, that the fox could not out run a turtle in a five-mile race. The other animals laughed at him and the turtle, as they bet on the fox. When the race started the fox took off down the road and out of sight. The other animals poked at the turtle and made fun of him as he slowly started the race. The fox came back and was taunting the turtle as he trudged along. The fox knew he could out run the turtle, so he would run ahead, stop and rest until the turtle caught up; then he would take off. The fox did this several times, as the turtle kept trudging along.

The fox started getting tired from running up and down the road; he was close to the finish line so he decided to take a quick nap. He stopped to rest, while the turtle kept plugging along. Of course the fox fell asleep. The turtle passed him and crossed the finish line. Somewhere in the twilight zone, the fox heard loud roars from the lion that woke him up. As the lion was collecting his money he was laughing and saying, "Only in America."

By: Dr. Romeo L. Taylor, Sr.

This story could have an effect on your life. One way of learning is to watch others. I'm sure you have had some foxes in your life. Maybe you have been a fox at sometime. In school, didn't you know some students that were destined to succeed in life because of their fast start? Have you tracked those students to see what happened to them?

You also knew some turtles, those students people said, "Would not amount to much." I'm sure things did not go quite the way people thought they would. As a matter of fact, many of the students I went to school with (before college) reversed their rolls when they entered the reality of life.

> "Don't let the lack of an advanced education discourage you from thinking great thoughts about better ways, that lack, may even be an advantage."
>
> by Joseph N. Jackson

New Attitude About Life

"Do what you've got to do, until you can do what you want to do." First be real with your self. Only push those things you can do. Pushing things you can't do is a waste of time.

Plan your future on paper. Spend your time on things that will progress you. Eliminate those persons in your life that are holding you back. Those friends of yours that have nothing to contribute towards progress, cut them loose. You can make it if you put forth the effort.

"Success comes from skillful planning"

DETERMINATION

"Let no one, place or thing,
Stop you from reaching
That place God has set aside for you."

By: Dr. Romeo L. Taylor, Sr.

I don't know what your position or condition is in life. Have you reached your goals or fulfilled your dreams? Have you allowed others to dictate or influenced your direction in life?

IT'S NEVER TOO LATE TO REACH YOUR GOALS

One of the major obstacles in reaching one's goals is the selection of friends, associates and mate.

Remember:

"Tough Times Don't Last,
But Tough People Do."

Author Unknown

"African Americans can continue to progress by Self-Pride, Self-Help, and Self-Determination."

By Leroy William Vaughn, M.D., M.B.A.

Chapter 16

BLACK PEOPLE IN RELIGION

Black Mary and the Christ Child

Many Black People we have talked to concerning this subject say, "What difference does it make?" We feel these people are still wrapped up in a slave mentality. It must have made a difference, for the White man to sell you the concept of a White Jesus for over 2,000 years.

We believe it would make a difference to the boy or girl in the ghetto that has lost hope. To the Black teenager that has been told for several years that they are worthless because they are Black; we are sure it would make a difference.

Jesus (the Christ) was Black. This is a fact. We're not talking about the concept of Jesus or the purpose of Jesus (the Christ) or his teaching. We are talking about the fact that, as a person who walked on this earth, he had a color. This color was not White, his color was the same as everyone else around him; BLACK.

Isn't it amazing how Black People in the United States have been studying the Holy Bible for all these years and have not determined for themselves that Jesus was Black.

Reading from, "THE BLACK MESSIAH," p. 3.

> "White Americans continue to insist upon a White Christ in the face of all historical evidence to the contrary and despite the hundreds of shrines to

> Black Madonna all over the world, is the growing, demonstrating of their White supremacist conviction that all things good and valuable must be White.
>
> On the other hand, until Black Christians are ready to challenge this lie, they have not freed themselves from their spiritual bondage to the White man nor established in their own minds their right to first class citizenship in Christ's Kingdom on earth.
>
> Black People cannot build dignity on their knees worshipping a White Christ. We must put down this White Jesus which the White man gave us in slavery and which has been tearing us to pieces."

Albert B. Cleage, Jr.

How long will Black People continue to be lead by other races?

> "Until Black People learn to face reality, act upon the reality we are facing, then do something to start controlling our destiny, we as a race will always be controlled by someone else."

Dr. BeLeTe

We have been so brain washed into believing information we receive from other people, it is almost like we have lost our ability to analyze information and draw our own conclusion. If you read it in a book see it in a newspaper, or hear it on the radio, it must be true. It may be true, true mind control.

The problem with many "so called educated Black People" is that they may not want to rock their boat of life. Therefore, they go along with the White society they associate with.

Dr. Carter Goodwin Woodson states:

> "When you control a man's thinking, you do not have to worry about his actions. You do not have to tell him not to stand here or go yonder. He will find his "proper place" and will stay in it. You do not need to send him to the back door. He will go without being told. In fact, it there is no back door, he will cut one for his special benefit. His education makes it necessary.
>
> "History show that it does not matter who is in power. Those who have not learned to do for themselves and have to depend solely on others never obtain any more right or privileges in the end, than they had in the beginning."

"The world has been deceived and lied to. It is time to set the record straight.

"The Bible is the best proof of the color of Jesus and most of the Biblical persons in the Old and New Testament were Black. See attached "Black People/Black Nations Of The Bible."

"The word Christ, comes from Indian, Krishna or Chrishna, which means, "The Black One."

"According to his own testimony, Christ Jesus himself is both "root and the offspring of David," (Revelation 22:15).

"God speaking to Ezekiel about the Jews in Chapter 16 verses 2 through 4 said, "Son of man, make known to Jerusalem: Your origin and your birth are of the land of the Canaanites; your father was an Amorite, and your mother a Hittite."

* * * * *

Reading "FROM BABYLON TO TIMBUKTU," Chapter IV, p. 33:

"Originally all Hamites and Shemites (or Semites) were black. Abraham was a black Shemite and a descendant of Shem. The name of Abraham was Abram, before he was referred to as Abraham. The three Hebrew patriarchs were Abraham, Isaac and Jacob. This Jacob begot twelve sons, who later fathered the twelve tribes of Israel. Abraham was the father not only of the Hebrew-Israelite nation, but also of the Arab nation.

"Now the mother and grandmother of the Arabian Nation were black Hamite Egyptian women, and the fathers of the Arabian nation were Abraham and Ishmael (Black Shemites).

"Josephus, the Jewish historian, wrote that Ishmael Married an Egyptian woman. As a result, he begot twelve sons. These twelve sons became twelve tribes and inhabited the region from the Euphrates to the Red Sea in the Arabian

Peninsula. This country is known today as Saudia Arabia. For those who do not believe that the ancient Arabians were black. If your mother and grandmother were Black, I am positive that you would have many colored features.

"Abraham, Isaac, Jacob, and the twelve tribes of Israel were all Black People. Jesus Christ was a Hebrew. Another point to prove that the Hebrews were Black is the Leprosy Laws, written in the thirteenth chapter of Leviticus. The strangest and most amazing phenomenon concerning biblical leprosy was that the skin turned White. Can a White man's skin turn White?

"The first chapter of the book of Matthew, Verses 1 through 17 gives the genealogy of Jesus Christ. Verse 1 says, "Jesus Christ the son of David, the son of Abraham."

We have already established that Abraham was Black. David was the father of King Solomon (both father and son were Black).

* * * * *

Reading from, "WHAT COLOR WAS JESUS?"

"The gospel of Matthew list three women who are noted as being ancestors of the Lord.

"The first woman is mentioned in Matthew 1:3 and is named Tamar. Tamar became an ancestor of Christ Jesus through a child she mothered by her own father-in-law Judah. The child's name was Perez (Mathew 1:3).

"The second woman is mentioned in Matthew 1:5 and is named Rahab. Her son "Boaz" was an ancestor of Christ Jesus, for she was Rahab the Canaanite (Matthew 1:5).

"The third woman who was a Black ancestor of Christ Jesus, mentioned in Matthew 1:6 is the "wife of Uriah," Bathsheba by name. Most know the story of David and Bathsheba. What is often overlooked is the fact that Bathsheba was married to Uriah the Hittite. It is widely known and accepted that the Hittites were a Hamitic people. They descended from Heth, a son of Canaan (Genesis 10:15, 13:10). If in fact Bathsheba shared the same ethnic origin as her husband (a not improbable assumption), then the child born to her and David, Solomon by name did indeed have Black ancestry in his veins. Solomon was an ancestor of Christ Jesus (Matthew 1:16).

"The blood relation of Mary to her forefather King David is collaborated by other Scriptures (see Luke 1:32, 69: Matthew 9:27; 15:22; 20:30; Mark 10:47, 48."

"Jesus was described in The Book of Revelations 1:14 and 1:15:

14. His head and his hair were White like wool, as White as snow; and his eyes were as a flame of fire;

15. And his feet like unto fine brass, as if they burned in a furnace, and his voice the sound of many waters

Without a doubt, the above information proves that Mary and Jesus Christ were nonwhite. Proving the above is simple, however, getting people to accept the truth will be the problem.

Read the King James Version of the Holy Bible with intelligence instead of emotions. For further information on the, "BLACK MARY AND CHRIST CHILD," Please read:

"WHAT COLOR WAS JESUS?"
by William Mosley

"SEX AND RACE" by J.A. Rogers

"THE BLACK MESSIAH" by Albert B. Cleage, Jr.

"WHAT THEY NEVER TOLD YOU IN HISTORY CLASS"
by Indus Knamit Kush

* * * * *

"The Saviors of Mankind, From Buddha to Jesus, Were Black"

"100 AMAZING FACTS ABOUT THE NEGRO" states,

> "Nearly all of the ancient gods of the Old and New World were Black and had wooly hair." Buckley says, "From the wooly texture of the hair I am inclined to assign to the Buddha of India; the Fuhi of China; the Xaha of the Japanese; and the Quetzalcoatl of the Mexicans, the same and indeed an African, or rather, a Nubian origin. In the Bible, God or the Ancient of Days, is

described as having "hair like the pure wool." The earliest statues of the Virgin Mary and Christ in Europe as far north as Russia, were Black and Negroid. Psalms that read like those of the Bible were written by Pharaoh, Amenophis IV, better known as "Akhenaton, the Heretic King," 1300 B.C. or more than 400 years before David was born. Akhenaton, who was the father of Tut-Ankh-Amen, was extremely Negro in type." We encourage you to read "100 AMAZING FACTS ABOUT THE NEGRO."

Even today, evidence can be found of this; see photos following.

"Black Madonna"
From Nuria, Spain is Called
"The Queen of the Pyrenees"

From "SEX & RACE"

- In Poland, she is called "The Black Madonna of Czestochowa."

- In Spain, there is a Black Madonna from Nuria called the "Queen of the Pyrenees."

- In Russia, Notre Dame of Kazar is a Black Virgin."

One can find a Black Christ:

- In France, the Cathedral of Millan;

- In Germany, the Cathedral of Augsburg;

- In Italy, the Church of San Francisco (at Pisa) as a Negro woman.

When Pope Pius was head of the Vatican State, an official postage stamp had the Virgin Mary as a Negro woman. Also, Spain had a postage stamp of its Black Virgin of Montserrat and Child.

* * * * *

Every year for the past 400 years, people from all over Central America come to Esquipulas, Guatemala to celebrate "Black Christ Day."

Press Telegram, January 16, 1999

* * * * *

Russia's Black Madonna
The Virgin of Kazan

BLACK PEOPLE / BLACK NATIONS OF THE BIBLE

– Compiled by Simon Burris

The earliest history of Black People dates back to the Book of Genesis in which Noah's three sons, Shem (name), Ham (black) and Japheth (fair) are described as the founders of the nations of the world.

The pages of the Bible are filled with over 2,000 names of persons, families, tribes, nations and other geographical locations of which pertain to many references of Black African identities.

Race as an identifying factor is not found in the Scriptures. Race or one's ethnicity usually was traced by and through a surname, ancestor, family tree, or national origin. The most common names identifying BLACKS or persons of BLACK AFRICAN ancestries during the Biblical days were: HAMITE, CUSHITE, HAGARITE, ISHMAELITE, SABEAN, PUTUTE, CYRENIAN, EGYPTIAN, ETHIOPIAN, SUDANESE, MIDIANITE, and a host of others. Post-AFRICAN-AMERICANS, AFRO-CUBAN, etc.

The following is a short list of BLACK PEOPLE AND BLACK NATIONS OF THE BIBLE, (with a brief biographical sketch of each). The literal meaning of each name is given in parentheses.

* * * * *

Old Testament

2300 BC, CUSH (black): The eldest son of HAM, grandson of Noah; his descendants (CUSHITES) peopled the areas of Southwest Asia, the Arabian Peninsula, ETHIOPIA, SUDAN and other areas of AFRICA.

Genesis 10: 7 - 12

EGYPT (land of HAM): A son of HAM, the BLACK founder of the country bearing his name, EGYPT, and forefather of the EGYPTIANS, BABYLONIANS (Iraqis), ARABIANS, CRETANS (southern Greeks), and the PHILISTINES (Palestinians).

Genesis 10: 12,14

PUT (bowman): A son of HAM, the founding father of the modern AFRICAN (Putute) nations of LIBYA (Cyrenaica), TUNISIA (Carthage), ALGERIA, MOROCCO and MAURITANIA.

Genesis 10:6

2218 BC, NIMROD (mighty): Son of CUSH, mighty hunter, the first great conqueror; founder of BABYLONIAN and ASSYRIAN empires (now modern Iraq).

Genesis 10:8 – 12

1914 BC, HAGAR (wandering): Sarah's EGYPTIAN AFRICAN handmaid, mother of Abraham's first son, ISHMAEL.

Genesis 16:1,15

1911 BC, ISHMAEL (whom God hears): Son of Abraham and his BLACK servant HAGAR; he married an AFRICAN woman, had 12 sons and several daughters.

Great ancestor of the many tribes and nations of the ISHMAELITES (Arabians).

Genesis 16:15; 25:12-18

1853 BC, KETURAH (fragrance): THE AFRICAN CUSHITE wife of Abraham after the death of Sarah. Their 5 sons became founders and rules of the BLACK CUSHITE kingdoms of SHEBA (Sabeans), today's YEMEN; DEDAN (Dedanites) and Nabatae (Nabataeans), the modern ARAB nations of SAUDI ARABIA, QATAR, KUWAIT, JORN AND BAHRAIN.

Genesis 25:1-4

1840 BC, MIDIAN (strife): A son of KETURAH and Abraham; ancestor and founder of the powerful nation of the MIDIANTES of SINAI, in EGYPT and western ARABIA. This nation existed for 30 centuries.

Genesis 25:1-4

1835 BC, KEDAR (black skinned): A son of ISHMAEL, founder of the kingdom of KEDAR (Kedarites), ARABIA.

Genesis 25:13

1760 BC, MAHALATH (mild) and BASEMATH (fragrant): Daughters of ISHMAEL, and wives of Esau, Jacob's twin brother.

Genesis 28:9; 36:3

1730 BC, POTIPHAR (belonging to the sun): The captain of the guard in Pharaoh's court. He purchased Joseph as a household slave from the ISHMAELITE traders to whom his brothers had sold him.

Genesis 39:1

POTIPHERA (like the sun): EGYPTIAN priest of the city of Heliopolis; father of ASENATH, Joseph's wife.

Genesis 41:45

1700 BC, MANASSEH (causing to forget): Oldest son of ASENATH and Joseph; BLACK founder of one of the 12 tribes of CANAAN/JUDAH.

Genesis 41:45; Chronicles 7:14-19

EPHRAIM (doubly fruitful): Second son of ASENATH and Joseph, brother of MANASSEH. Ancestor of the CANAANITE tribe bearing his name.

Genesis 41:52; I Chronicles 7:20 - 27

1530 BC, JETHRO (his excellence): A BLACK priest of MIDIAN, Moses married his daughter, ZIPPORAH.

Exodus 3:1

ZIPPORAH (little bird): Daughter of JETHRO, wife of Moses, and mother of GERSHOM and ELIEZER.

Exodus 18:1-4

1501 BC, King THUTMOSE and Queen HATSHEPSUT were rulers of
1447 BC, EGYPT during the Exodus period.

Exodus 1:8; 2:5

SHIPHRAH (splendid) and PUAH (glitter): The two EGYPTIAN midwives of the Hebrews who disobeyed the command of Pharaoh to kill the Hebrew male children.

Exodus 1:15

1490 BC, ELISHAMA (God has heard): Leader in the wilderness of SINAI under Moses' command; a descendant of ASENATH; grandfather of Joshua.

1451 BC, JOSHUA (Jehovah is salvation): Successor of Moses as leader; led the Israelites in invasion and settlement of Canaan (Israel). His BLACK ancestry can be traced through his AFRICAN EPHRAIMITE lineage: NUN, ELISHAMA, EPHRAIM, to ASENATH, the BLACK wife of Joseph.

Exodus 17:9

1406 BC, JONATHAN (Jehovah's gift): Grandson of Moses and ZIPPORAH, who after the death of JOSHUA, served as a priest, first of Micah, and then to the tribe of Dan. He and his sons were priest until the fall of the Northern Kingdom of Israel in 712 BC.

Judges 18:19,30

1394 BC, CUSHAN-RISHATHAIM (Ethiopian of double wickedness): CUSHITE King of Mesopotamia; he ruled over the Israelites for 8 years until one of the first judges, JOSHUA, led a successful rebellion against him.

Judges 3:8

1249 BC, OREB (raven) and ZEEB (wolf): ETHIOPIAN MIDIANITE princes and leaders of the great invasion of Israel.

Judges 7:25

1209 BC, ABIMELECH (father of the king): A son of judge Gideon by an ISHMAELITE woman of Shechem; he was elected king of the independent state of Shechem, in Israel; first to try to make Israel a kingdom.

Judges 8:31, 9 – 6

1048 BC, JETHER (abundance): An ISHMAELITE; married King David's sister, Abigail.

I Chronicles 2:17

1025 BC, SHEBUEL (captive of God): Grandson of Moses and KETURAH, his CUSHITE wife; was King David's treasurer.

I Chronicles 26:24

1023 BC, AMASA (burden bearer): Son of JETHER, the ISHMAELITE, and David's sister Abigail, who Absalom made captain over his rebel army.

2 Samuel 17:25

1000 BC, TAHPENES (grandeur): The Queen of Egypt who gave asylum to Hadad of Edom who escaped the murdering of the Edomites carried out by Joab, David's general.

I Kings II

995 BC, Queen of SHEBA (an oath): The BLACK ARABIAN Queen visited King Solomon; she presented gifts to him containing almost 5 tons of gold and a very large amount of spices and jewels.

I Kings 10:1 – 13

975 BC, SHISHAK (the Putite): First LIBYAN Pharaoh of EGYPT; he invaded and captured Jerusalem and Southern Judah during the reign of King Rehoboam.

I Kings 14:25,26

941 BC, ZERAH (rising of light): Ethiopian king and commander; Invaded Judah with an army of a million men, including 300 chariots, and marched to within 25 miles of Jerusalem.

I Chronicles 14:9

728 BC, SO: King of EGYPT, of Ethiopian descent; his alliance was sought for by Hosea, the last King of Israel.

2 Kings 17:4

726 BC, TIRHARKAH (exhalted): The last Ethiopian Pharaoh of EGYPT; king of ETHIOPIA and the SUDAN.

2 Kings 19:9

640 BC, ZEPHANIAH (whom God hid): Son of CUSHI, the ETHIOPIAN;

610 BC, NECHO (holy): A Pharaoh of EGYPT; he defeated and killed

609 BC, a BLACK prophet in the days of Josiah, whose Book of Prophecies still remains.

Zephaniah 1:1

595 BC, Josiah, King of Judah of Megiddo; controlled Syria and Palestine until about 605 BC.

2 Kings 23:29

589 BC, EBEDMELECH (servant of the king): The EGYPTIAN guardian in the service of King Zedekiah, through whose aid Jeremiah was released from prison.

Jeremiah 38:7 - 13

588 BC - HOPHRA (crocodile): Pharaoh of EGYPT, the second successor

570 BC, after NECHO, and the last Pharaoh mentioned in the Scriptures.

Jeremiah 44:30

New Testament

00 AD, Mary Mother of Jesus. See Black Mary and Christ Child, above.

29 AD, SIMON of CYRENE (hearing): From LIBYA in AFRICA, he carried the cross for Jesus on the road to Calvary.

Matthew 27:32

33 AD, The ETHIOPIAN prime minister (treasurer) converted and baptized by Philip, the evangelist, on his way back from Jerusalem to ETHIOPIA.

Acts 8:27

36 AD, CANDACE (of MEROE): Queen of ETHIOPIA.

Acts 11:20

36 AD, Christian converts from CYRENE in AFRICA.

Acts 11:20

48 AD, SIMEON (hearing) called NIGER (black): A Christian prophet and teacher in the church at Antioch, in Syria.

Acts 13:1

48 AD, Lucius (light) of CYRENE: An AFRICAN prophet and teacher in the first Gentile Christian church at Antioch.

Acts 13:1

54 - 57 AD, APOLLOS (destroyer): An EGYPTIAN AFRICAN, he was an eloquent and learned Christian missionary, teacher, preacher, and orator at Ephesus, Asia Minor (Turkey) and Corinth (Greece); an aide to Saint Paul. Tradition makes him Bishop of Caesarea, in Palestine.

Acts 18:24-28; 19:1

ALEXANDER (helper of man) and RUFUS (red): Sons of SIMON of CYRENE; Christian missionaries in Jerusalem.

Mark 15:21

* * * * *

Bibliographical Sources

THE HOLY BIBLE (King James Version)

Secondary References

OXFORD'S NEW STANDARD JEWISH ENCYCLOPEDIA (1992)

Peloubel, F.N., "BIBLE DICTIONARY" (1922)

WEBSTER'S BIOGRAPHICAL DICTIONARY (1953)

Young, Robert, "ANALYTICAL CONCORDANCE TO THE BIBLE" (1912)

Chapter 17

DID YOU KNOW ?

1. The city named Beverly Hills, California was once called Rancho Rodeo de Las Aguas and was owned by Maria Rita Valdez, whose black grandparents were among the founding members of Los Angeles.

2. The San Fernando Valley in California was owned by Francisco Reyes, a Black Man. Francisco Reyes became the first Black Mayor of Los Angeles.

3. Pio Pico, whose grandmother was a mulatto, was the last governor of California under Mexican control, from 1845-1846. Pico Boulevard in Los Angeles and Pico Rivera, California are both named after him.

4. Dr. Caesar, an original slave from Africa, developed a cure for poisons in 1792. He was only known as Doctor.

5. An African Prince, Prince Hall founded Black Masonry and formed the first Negro Grand Lodge; "African Grand Lodge of North America." After his death, the name was changed to "Prince Hall Grand Lodge, F. & A. M. of Massachusetts."

6. The first person to die in the American Revolution during the Boston massacre in 1770 was a free Black Man.

7. In 1999, America's drug users were 12% black, 70% White. Check the book, "Don't Believe the Hype," by Farai Chideya.

8. There was a real Ol' Saint Nick who had an African partner named Pete. St Nick lived over 1,000 years ago. Each year he and Pete would travel from Jerusalem to Holland and give presents away to children. The story of this gift-giving duo is told in the book, "Santa and Pete' by Christopher Moore and Pamela Johnson.

9. Bill Pickett was the first Black Cowboy inducted into the Rodeo Hall of Fame. He is credited with inventing the bulldogging event (steer wrestling).

10. The word "cowboy" originated from what the White people called Blacks that worked with cows.

11. NEVER USE THE WORD "PICNIC." Every Friday, the KKK, White supremacists and mobs, would pick-a-nigger to either hang or burn at the stake. They called this a picnic and it went on for years in Southern states and elsewhere around the nation.

12. The first historically black college was founded in Philadelphia in 1832 as the institute for Colored Youth. It is now called Cheyney State University.

13. Otis Boykin, in 1955, invented a regulating unit for the first heart pacemaker.

An Electric Light Bulb
From a Carving 2,500 B.C. at Dendra, Egypt

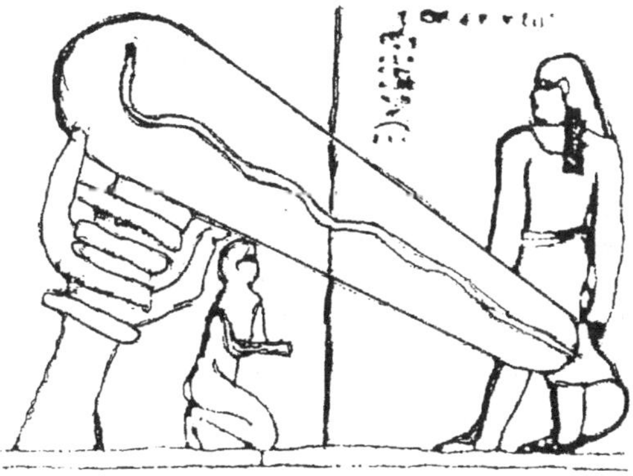

It is known that the ancient world used electric current generated by efficient little batteries which were probably used for electroplating metals with gold or silver. Reconstructions of these primitive batteries reveal they could produce about 2.5 volts each. Connected in series, they might have lit the six-foot light bulb shown in the carving. The serpent-like filament held up by high-tension insulators, from which run braided cables, connected to what is clearly a transformer of some kind, could have had a brilliance equal to the headlamp of a modern car.

14. Y Chromosome shows that Adam (in the Bible) was African

"SCIENCE" by Ann Gibbons, 1997

15. Scientists isolate Neanderthal DNA from fossil. Researchers conclude, "Humans aren't creature's direct descendants."

Sue Goetinck,
Writer for The Dallas Morning News
July 11, 1997

16. Genetic evidence points to African origin of humans.

Reuters, March 31, 1997

17. African Woman Mother Of Us All.

Contemporary Woman's Issues Database
June 1, 1994

18. During the so-called slavery days, White folks had a laughing barrel. If they caught a Black person laughing, they had to put their head in the barrel, and get kicked in the ass.

19. During the Second World War, White solders would tell the White women in London that, after midnight, Black solders would grow "tails."

20. Sears and Roebuck was started by two people, one White and one Black. Guess which was Black? Roebuck was Black. What happened to him?

21. J. Ernest Wilkins, Ph.D. and Lloyd Quartman were among the six Black scientists who helped in the making of the first Atomic bomb (code-named the Manhattan Project).

22. Lloyd Quartman also helped develop the first nuclear reactor that was used in the atomic powered submarine called the Nautilus.

23. Jean Baptiste Point Du Sable was the founder of the city of Chicago, in the 18th century.

24. Frederick Gregory was the first Black man to pilot a space shuttle and the third Black man to go into space.

25. Jim Beckwourth (Black Mountain Man) became Chief of the Crow Indians and founder of the city of Denver, Colorado.

26. The creator of "The Three Musketeers" was a Black man named Alexander Dumas.

27. Black People as a race, spend nearly $700 billion per year; especially on entertainment, which does not return to the community.

28. Bridget "Biddy" Mason, was the first Black female property owner in Los Angeles, California, owning much of Spring Street in downtown. She was also founder of the First African Methodist Episcopal (AME) Church.

* * * * *

The Africoid Olmecs Were the Parent Culture of Ancient America

Flourishing more than 1,000 years before Christ, the Olmecs were the parent civilization of Ancient America. Colossal monuments of stone heads in Mexico show numerous carvings of them as gods. Their faces are unmistakably Africoid, and their hair is plaited or in corn rows! Further, they were Twa (Pygmies). There are many Africoid portraits in stone, clay, copper and gold. In addition to their early culture-shaping role, the Olmecs were undoubtedly profoundly influenced by Black migrants from Africa's Nile Valley. Columbus himself made emphatic reference to Black traders from Guinea.

Afrikan Technology Built Mexico's Pyramids and More

The reason for the profound similarity between ancient Middle American and Kamit is because Kamit authored that civilization, including Mexico's pyramids.

Did Afrikans Also Rule All of South and Central America?

Yes! According to Peruvian historian, Eduardo de Habiche who documents this in his Spanish book, "EL PERU MILENARIO DES QUICIA LAS BASES DE LA: HISTORIA UNIVERSAL" (Lima, Peru 1983). He asserts that these Afrikans were Egyptian invaders seeking Peruvian gold.

Taken From A Handout
Author Unknown

Pictures of Ancient Black Gods in America

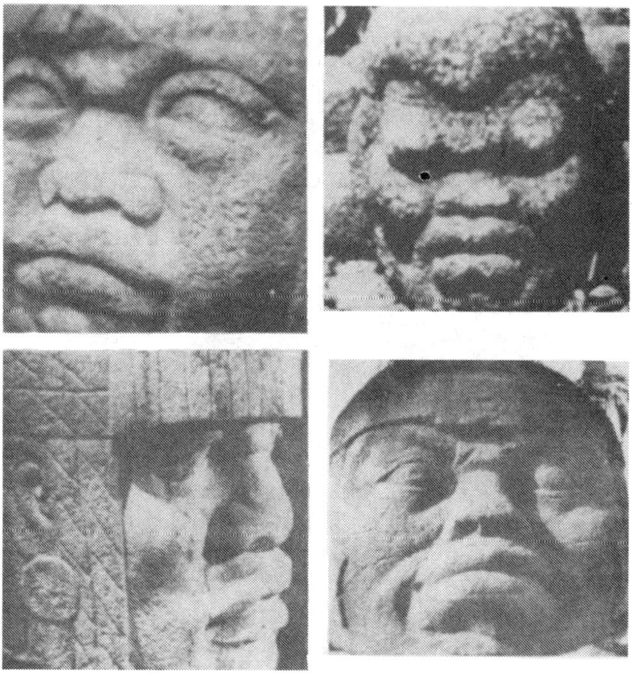

From “THE BLACK BOOK:”

Colonel A. Braghine said that he saw in a collection in Ecuador a statuette of a Negro that is at least “20,000 years old.” He adds, “Some statues of the Indian gods in Central America possess typical Negro features and certain prehistoric monuments there undoubtedly represent “Negroes.”

Read: ‘THE SHADOW OF ATLANTIS, pp. 40-42

Black God of Ancient America

Head of Olmec Deity

Weight about five tons.
From full-size reproduction in the
American Museum of Natural History
in New York

Chapter 18

"THOUGHTS" - PART I

By Dr. Romeo L. Taylor, Sr.
© 2003

I HAVE A DREAM
BUT A DREAM
WITHOUT A PLAN AND EXECUTION,
REMAINS NOTHING BUT A DREAM.
By Dr. Romeo L. Taylor, Sr.

I SAY
THEY SAY, "KNOWLEDGE IS POWER"
By Jean-Paul Sartre
I SAY, "KNOWLEDGE SHARED AND APPLIED,
IS POWER.
KNOWLEDGE NOT SHARED NOR APPLIED
IS WASTED."
By Dr. Romeo L. Taylor, Sr.

REALITY
MANS CHOICE TO BELIEVE OR NOT,
ACCEPT OR NOT, DOES NOT CHANGE
THE REALITY OF ANYTHING IN THE UNIVERSE.
By Dr. Romeo L. Taylor, Sr.

HE SAID
HE SAID,"WITHOUT STRUGGLE, THERE IS NO
PROGRESS".
By Frederick Douglas
I SAY,"WITHOUT MOTIVATION, THERE IS NO
STRUGGLE".
By Dr. Romeo L. Taylor, Sr.

CHANGE IN LIFE

WITHOUT A CHANGE IN YOUR ACTIONS,
THERE CAN BE NO CHANGE IN YOUR LIFE.

By: Dr. Romeo L. Taylor, Sr.

MESSAGE FROM THE GHETTO

HELP ME TO HELP MYSELF,
FOR I SHALL SURVIVE.

By Dr. Romeo L. Taylor, Sr.

FROM START TO FINISH

SUCCESS EQUALS,
THE KNOWLEDGE AND
EFFORT IN BETWEEN.

By Dr. Romeo L. Taylor, Sr.

DIVINE CREATION

YOU ARE WHAT GOD CREATED,
MAKE THE MOST OF IT.

By Dr. Romeo L. Taylor, Sr.

DETERMINATION

LET NO ONE, PLACE OR THING
STOP YOU FROM REACHING
THAT PLACE, GOD HAS SET
ASIDE FOR YOU.

By Dr. Romeo L. Taylor, Sr.

MONEY

THE EVIDENCE OF THE TRUE WANT
AND NEED OF MONEY
IS SHOWN IN THE EFFORT
TO GET IT.

By Dr. Romeo Taylor, Sr.

TIME

UNPRODUCTIVE TIME IS A
WASTE OF LIFE.

By Dr. Romeo L. Taylor, Sr.

LOSS IN LIFE

TIME IS THE BIGGEST
LOSS IN LIFE.

By Dr. Romeo L. Taylor, Sr.

SUCCESS

SUCCESS COMES FROM
SKILLFUL PLANNING.

By Dr. Romeo L. Taylor, Sr.

SLAVERY

THE 13TH AMENDMENT OF THE US CONSTITUTION
BROKE THE PHYSICAL CHAINS OF SLAVERY.
LET KNOWLEDGE OVERCOME SLAVE MENTALITY.

By Dr. Romeo L. Taylor, Sr.

ILLUSION

SOMETIMES LIFE CAN BE AN ILLUSION,
FOR EVERYTHING YOU SEE
MAY NOT BE WHAT YOU PERCEIVE IT TO BE.

By Dr. Romeo L. Taylor, Sr.

TRUTH

HOW CAN ONE DETERMINE THE TRUTH,
WHEN THE CONSPIRACY IS TO PROMOTE
UNTRUTHS?

By Dr. Romeo L. Taylor, Sr.

GOD'S CHOICE

NEVER QUESTION GODS' REASON FOR ANYTHING!
ACCEPT. ADJUST YOUR LIFE AND MOVE ON.
HIS PLAN IS STILL WORKING.

By Dr. Romeo L. Taylor, Sr.

BUSINESS

BE SURE YOUR BUSINESS
WORKS FOR YOU,
INSTEAD OF YOU WORKING
FOR THE BUSINESS.

By Dr. Romeo L. Taylor, Sr.

KEEP WATCHING

WHAT PEOPLE SAY,
IS NOT AS IMPORTANT
AS WHAT THEY DO.
KEEP WATCHING.

By Dr. Romeo L. Taylor, Sr.

LIFE

LIFE IS LIKE A TV SET.
IF YOU DON'T LIKE WHAT
YOU ARE LOOKING AT,
CHANGE THE CHANNEL!

By Dr. Romeo L. Taylor, Sr.

HUMAN BEINGS

NO MATTER WHAT ONE SAYS OR DOES,
EVERYONE ALIVE CAN BE NOTHING MORE THAN
A HUMAN BEING.
GOD DID NOT CREATE ANY SAINTS.

By Dr. Romeo L. Taylor, Sr.

"THOUGHTS" - PART II

By Dr. Romeo L. Taylor, Sr.
© 2003

FOREVER YOURS

THE LONGEVITY OF LOVE
IS APPRECIATION.
By Dr. Romeo L. Taylor, Sr.

YOU HAVE NOTHING

THEY SAY, "I LOVE YOU," OR "I'M YOUR FRIEND,"
BUT LOVE AND FRIENDSHIP,
WITHOUT SUBSTANCE, IS NOTHING.
By Dr. Romeo L. Taylor, Sr.

NOTHING TO LOSE

WHEN YOU HAVE NOTHING, TRY ANYTHING,
CAUSE YOU HAVE NOTHING TO LOSE.
By Dr. Romeo L. Taylor, Sr.

HE LIVES

THE EVIDENCE OF A LIVING GOD,
IS SHOWN EVERYDAY,
BY THE MIRACLES HE PERFORMS.
By Dr. Romeo L. Taylor, Sr.

MOST IMPORTANT

THEY SAY, "YOUR HOUSE AND CAR ARE
YOUR BIGGEST INVESTMENTS IN LIFE."
I SAY, "YOUR HEALTH SHOULD BE YOUR
BIGGEST INVESTMENT IN LIFE."
By Dr. Romeo L. Taylor, Sr.

FINISH STRONG

IT'S NOT AS IMPORTANT
WHERE YOU START OFF IN LIFE,
BUT WHERE YOU FINISH.
THERE ARE THOSE THAT START OFF STRONG,
ONLY TO DROP IN THE LONG RUN.
THERE ARE THOSE THAT START OFF SLOW OR LATE,
BUT FINISH STRONG.
KEEP YOUR COURSE, IT'S NEVER TOO LATE

By Dr. Romeo L. Taylor, Sr.

STORM

SOMETIMES LIFE IS LIKE A STORM,
IF YOU CAN'T TAKE IT,
YOU CAN'T MAKE IT.

By Dr. Romeo L. Taylor, Sr.

WASTED LIFE

"A LIFE IS A TERRABLE THING TO WASTE,"
IT'S NEVER TOO LATE TO PROGRESS.
TAKE CONTROL, ELIMINATE THOSE THINGS
AND PEOPLE, THAT HOLD YOU DOWN.
REMEMBER GOD HAS A PLAN FOR YOU.
BE GUIDED BY YOUR SPRIT,
AND YOU CAN OVER COME ANYTHING.

By Dr. Romeo L. Taylor, Sr.

FROM BIRTH

NO ONE IS BORN
A THUG OR CRIMINAL.
CONDITIONS OF LIFE
BREED THEM.

By Dr. Romeo L. Taylor, Sr.

TALKING

DEVELOP THE ABILITY TO
"TALK A LITTLE, YET SAY A LOT"
INSTEAD OF
"TALKING A LOT AND SAYING A LITTLE"
By Dr. Romeo L. Taylor, Sr.

IT'S REAL

FACTS ARE FACTS,
WHETHER YOU BELIEVE THEM OR NOT.
By Dr. Romeo L. Taylor, Sr.

TO LEARN

LISTEN AND READ WITH INTELLENCE,
INSTEAD OF EMOTIONS.
By Dr. Romeo L. Taylor, Sr.

YOU CAN MAKE IT

IF YOU START WITH NOTHING, TAKE GOD,
PREPARE A PLAN, AND GO!
YOU CAN MAKE IT IF YOU TRY.
By Dr. Romeo L. Taylor, Sr.

JUSTICE

JUSTICE IS ONLY EQUAL WHEN YOU
HAVE EQUAL KNOWLEDGE AND
EQUAL REPRESENTATION!
By Dr. Romeo L. Taylor, Sr.

IGNORANCE

IGNORANCE IS A FORM,
OF SELF-IMPOSED SLAVERY.
By Dr. Romeo L. Taylor, Sr.

CONTROL

YOU MAY HAVE CONTROL OF A PERSON'S BODY,
BUT YOU CANNOT CONTROL THEIR MIND.

By: Dr. Romeo L. Taylor, Sr.

THINKING

YOU ARE AND WILL BE WHAT YOU THINK.
POSITIVE THINKING ALONG WITH POSITIVE ACTIONS,
CAN PRODUCE A POSITIVE LIFESTYLE.

By: Dr. Romeo L. Taylor, Sr.

CHANGE IN LIFE

WITHOUT A CHANGE IN YOUR ACTIONS,
THERE CAN BE NO CHANGE IN YOUR LIFE.

By: Dr. Romeo L. Taylor, Sr.

* * * * *

Chapter 19

IN CONCLUSION

We hope that everyone reading this book reads it with intelligence instead of emotions. The purpose of this book was to correct lies that have been told for centuries concerning the contributions of Black People to civilization. To bury any and all studies whose results revealed that Black intelligence was lower than other races (especially the White race). To inform Black People of true Black History around the world, especially in the United States.

This book was not written to put any other race down, but to life the Black race up to its proper stature in life.

Blacks have been misled into chasing civil rights, when they should have been after economic rights.

The fueling of racism has been a diversion by the people in power, so both Blacks and Whites don't concentrate on other things that are going on in the world.

We need to develop a new attitude for progress. We must first clean up our own house before we can deal with other homes.

Brothers and sisters, it's later than you think. If we do not pull together NOW, in 20 years there will be nothing left for us.

For those Blacks who were not aware of the information in this book, you should be proud to know your ancestors achieved as much as they did. Every Black person should know the information contained in this book and face reality.

> "NO RACE OR GROUP OF PEOPLE WILL HELP US, IF WE AS A RACE, DON'T WAKE UP AND HELP OURSELVES."
>
> Dr. BeLeTe

We must face the facts . . .

As the Past President Botha of South Africa stated:

> "It is comforting to know that behind the scenes, Europe, America, Canada, Australia all and others are behind us, in spite of what they say. For diplomatic relations, we all know what language should be used and where."

WE SHOULD REMEMBER HIS WORDS "FOREVER."

* * * * *

KEEP WATCHING
WHAT PEOPLE SAY
IS NOT AS IMPORTANT
AS WHAT THEY DO.
KEEP WATCHING!
By: Dr. Romeo L. Taylor, Sr.

* * * * *

Every time lawmakers say one thing, and do something else, we should remember, it's part of their game. How long will we go along with their games? Now should be the days of accountability.

> "When you control a man's thinking, you do not have to worry about his actions you do not have to tell him not to stand here or go yonder. He will find his proper place, and will stay in it. You do not have to send him to the back door. He will go without being told. In fact, if there is no back door, he will cut one for his special benefit. His education makes it necessary.
>
> "History shows that it does not matter who is in power... those who have not learned to do for themselves and have to depend solely on others never obtain any more rights or privileges in the end than they had in the beginning."
>
> Dr. Carter G. Woodson

As a race, we have been manipulated into believing we are doing well. Are we? Give this a thought, Black newspapers are still on the once a week delivery (Thursdays ONLY!). It's been that way for centuries. Blacks only own a few first-run movie theaters in the United States. Thousands of Black People go to the movies weekly in theaters owned by someone else. With all the money Black entertainers and sport figures are making, where are the black owned banks, hotels or large commercial buildings?

Even though Black entertainers and sport figures are making big bucks, who controls their money? Who is making the decision on their investments? This may indicate what's going on behind the scenes. As stated before, "We grow up putting our money in the hands of other races." When will the cycle stop? We're sure there are Black professional money managers, qualified to manage money for Black professionals.

Black professional people should set aside 5% of their taxable income and direct this money towards Black progress.

I'm sure several Black professionals could go together, or individually, purchase a 5-star hotel and set it up as a training program for minorities to learn hotel and restaurant management. They could also provide a training program for chefs. This would provide a lot of jobs. Such a program could get government funding. Think about it.

Once a person is financially secured for life and has everything they want and need, what's left for them to do with money but help others. People in high tax brackets pay a lot in taxes, however, they can legally establish foundations and charities which would reduce their tax base. Through these establishments, they can make money available for Black progress. They can actually help their people, without it costing them anything. Other races have been doing this for years. Who's managing Black dollars?

* * * * *

We leave you with a few thoughts:

1. Truly love one another. Without love there is no future. There are a lot of Black People who are lost, because of the lack of true love. Take time to be courteous to one another, for in the end we will only have ourselves. Men, love and respect your women. Women love and respect your men for you truly may only have each other.

2. Stop living in a cloud. Face the facts as they are presented. Black People are always talking about we need to get together. Now is the time, stop talking and start acting. What's here today will not be here tomorrow.

3. Learn, Baby, Learn. We must understand that, "Ignorance is a form of self imposed slavery," because you must always depend on someone else to direct you. The time has come where we must get down to serious business. We must push away all those things that have been pushed into our communities to destroy us. Black leaders need to lead and stop going along with programs that don't benefit us now or in the future. Black leaders must understand when they are no longer needed by the power structure, they are dumped. Many good people have been dumped by the wayside, because they refused to believe it would happen to them.

The 13th Amendment of the United States Broke the Physical Chains of Slavery.

Let Knowledge Overcome Slave Mentality!

Dr. Romeo Taylor, Sr.
Hotep (Peace)

Chapter 20

DOCUMENTS OF THE UNITED STATES OF AMERICA

Articles of Confederation

I.
The Style of this Confederacy shall be
"THE UNITED STATES OF AMERICA"

II.
Each state retains its sovereignty, freedom, and independence, and every power, jurisdiction, and right, which is not by this Confederation expressly delegated to the United States, in Congress assembled.

III.
The said States hereby severally enter into a firm league of friendship with each other, for their common defense, the security of their liberties, and their mutual and general welfare, binding themselves to assist each other, against all force offered to, or attacks made upon them, or any of them, on account of religion, sovereignty, trade, or any other pretense whatever.

IV.
The better to secure and perpetuate mutual friendship and intercourse among the people of the different States in this Union, the free inhabitants of each of these States, paupers, vagabonds, and fugitives from justice excepted, shall be entitled to all privileges and immunities of free citizens in the several states; and the people of each State shall have free ingress and regress to and from any other State, and shall enjoy therein all privileges of trade and commerce, subject to the same duties, impositions, and restrictions as the inhabitants

thereof respectively, provided that such restrictions shall not extend so far as to prevent the removal of property imported into any State, to any other State, of which the owner is an inhabitant; provided also that no imposition, duties or restriction shall be laid by any State, on the property of the United States, or either of them.

If any person guilty of or charged with, treason, felony, or other high misdemeanor in any State, shall flee from justice, and be found in any of the United States, he shall, upon demand of the governor or executive power of the State from which he fled, be delivered up and removed to the State having jurisdiction of his offense.
Full faith and credit shall be given in each of these States to the records, acts, and judicial proceedings of the courts and magistrates of every other State.

V.
For the most convenient management of the general interests of the United States, delegates shall be annually appointed in such manner as the legislatures of each State shall direct, to meet in Congress on the first Monday in November, in every year, with a power; reserved to each State to recall its delegates, or any of them, at any time within the year, and send others in their stead for the remainder of the year.

No state shall be represented in Congress by less than two, nor more than seven members; and no person shall be capable of being a delegate for more than three years in any term of six years; nor shall any person, being a delegate, be capable of holding any office under the United States, for which he, or another for his benefit, receives any salary, fees or emolument of any kind.
Each State shall maintain its own delegates in a meeting

of the States, and while they act as members of the committee of the States.

In determining questions in the United States, in Congress assembled, each State shall have one vote.
Freedom of speech and debate in Congress shall not be impeached or questioned in any court or place out of Congress, and the members of Congress shall be protected in their persons from arrests and imprisonments, during the time of their going to and from, and attendance on Congress, except for treason, felony, or breach of the peace.

VI.

No State, without the consent of the United States in Congress assembled, shall send any embassy to, or receive any embassy from, or enter into any conference, agreement, alliance or treaty with any King, Prince or State; nor shall any person holding any office of profit or trust under the United States, or any of them, accept of any present, emolument, office or title of any kind whatever from any King, Prince or foreign State; nor shall the United States in Congress assembled, or any of them, grant any title of nobility.

No two or more States shall enter into any treaty, confederation or alliance whatever between them, without the consent of the United States in Congress assembled, specifying accurately the purposes for which the same is to be entered into, and how long it shall continue.

No State shall lay any imposts or duties, which may interfere with any stipulations in treaties, entered into by the United States in Congress assembled, with any

King, Prince or State, in pursuance of any treaties already proposed by Congress, to the courts of France and Spain.

No vessel of war shall be kept up in time of peace by any State, except such number only, as shall be deemed necessary by the United States in Congress assemble, for the defense of such State, or its trade; nor shall any body of forces be kept up by any State in time of peace, except such number only, as in the judgement of the United States in Congress assembled, shall be deemed requisite to garrison the forts necessary for the defense of such State; but every State shall always keep up a well-regulated and disciplined militia, sufficiently armed and accoutered, and shall provide and constantly have ready for use, in public stores, a due number of field pieces and tents, and a proper quantity of arms, ammunition and camp equipage.

No State shall engage in any war without the consent of the United States in Congress assembled, unless such State be actually invaded by enemies, or shall have received certain advice of a resolution being formed by some nation of Indians to invade such State, and the danger is so imminent as not to admit of a delay, till the United States in Congress assembled can be consulted; nor shall any State grant commissions to any ships or vessels of war, nor letters of marque or reprisal, except it be after a declaration of war by the United States in Congress assembled, and then only against the Kingdom or State and the subjects thereof, against which war has been so declared, and under such regulations as shall be established by the United States in Congress assembled, unless such State be infested by pirates, in which case vessels of war be fitted out for that occasion, and kept so long as the danger shall continue, or until the United States in Congress assembled shall determine otherwise.

VII.

When land forces are raised by any State for the common defense, all officers of or under the rank of colonel, shall be appointed by the legislature of each State respectively, by whom such forces shall be raised, or in such manner as such State shall direct, all vacancies shall be filled up by the State which first made the appointment.

VIII.

All charges of war, and all other expenses that shall be incurred for the common defense or general welfare, and allowed by the United States in Congress assembled, shall be defrayed out of a common treasury, which shall be supplied by the several States in proportion to the value of all land within each State, granted to surveyed for any person, as such land and the buildings and improvements thereon shall be estimated according to such mode as the United States in Congress assembled, shall from time to time direct and appoint.

The taxes for paying that proportion shall be laid and levied by the authority and direction of the legislatures of the several States within the time agreed upon by the United States in Congress assembled.

IX.

The United States in Congress assembled, shall have the sole and exclusive right and power of determining on peace and war, expect in the cases mentioned in the sixth article, of sending and receiving ambassadors, entering into treaties and alliances, provided that no treaty of commerce shall be made whereby the legislative power of the respective States shall be restrained from imposing such imposts and duties on foreigners, as their own people are subjected to, or from prohibiting the exportation or importation of any species of goods or commodities whatsoever; of establishing rules for deciding in all cases, what captures on land or water shall be legal, and in what manner prizes taken by land or naval forces in the service of the United States shall be divided or appropriated; of granting letters of marque and reprisal in times of peace; appointing courts for the trial of piracies and felonies committed on the high seas and establishing courts for receiving and determining finally appeals in all cases of captures, provided that no member of Congress shall be appointed a judge of any of the said courts.

The United States in Congress assembled shall also be the last resort or appeal in all disputes and differences now subsisting or that hereafter may arise between two or more States concerning boundary, jurisdiction or any other causes whatever; which authority shall always be exercised in the manner following. Whenever the legislative or executive authority or lawful agent of any State in controversy with another shall present a petition to Congress stating the matter in question and praying for a hearing, notice thereof shall be given by order of Congress to the legislative or executive authority of the other State in controversy, and a day assigned for the appearance of the parties by their lawful agents, who shall then be directed to appoint by joint consent, commissioners or judges to constitute a court for hearing and determining the matter in question: but if they cannot agree, Congress shall name three persons out of each of the United States, and from the list of such persons each party shall alternately strike out one, the petitioners beginning, until the number shall be reduced to thirteen; and from that number not less than seven, nor more than nine names, as Congress shall direct, shall in the presence of Congress be drawn out by lot, and the persons whose names shall be so drawn or any five of them, shall be commissioners or judges, to hear and finally determine the controversy, so always as a major part of the judges, who shall hear the cause shall agree in the determination: and if either party shall neglect to attend at the day appointed, without showing reasons, which Congress shall judge sufficient, or being present shall refuse to strike, the Congress shall proceed to nominate three persons out of each State, and the Secretary of Congress shall strike in behalf of such party absent or refusing; and the judgment and sentence of the court to be appointed, in the manner before prescribed, shall be final and conclusive; and if any of the parties shall refuse to submit to the authority of such court, or to appear or defend their claim or cause, the court shall nevertheless proceed to pronounce sentence, or judgement, which shall in like manner be final and decisive, the judgement or sentence and other proceedings being in either case transmitted to Congress, and lodged among the acts of Congress for the security of the parties concerned: provided that every commissioner, before he sits in judgement, shall take an oath to be administered by one of the judges of the supreme or superior court of the State, where the cause shall be tried, "well and truly to hear and determine the matter in question, according to the best of his judgement, without favor, affection or hope of reward" provided also, that no State shall be deprived of territory for the benefit of the United States.

All controversies concerning the private right of soil claimed under different grants of two or more States, whose jurisdictions as they may respect such lands, and the States which passed such grants are adjusted, the said grants or either of them being at the same time claimed to have originated antecedent to such settlement of jurisdiction, shall on the petition of either party to the Congress of the United States, be finally determined as near as may be in the same manner as is before prescribed for deciding disputes respecting territorial jurisdiction between different States.

The United States in Congress assembled shall also have the sole and exclusive right and power of regulating the alloy and value of coin struck by their own authority, or by that of the respective States – fixing the standards of weights and measures throughout the United States, regulating the trade and managing all affairs with the Indians, not members of any of the States, provided that the legislative right of any State within its own limits be not infringed or violated, establishing or regulating post offices from one State to another, throughout all the United States, and exacting such postage on the papers passing through the same as may be requisite to defray the expenses of the said office; appointing all officers of the land forces, in the service of the United States, excepting regimental officers; appointing all the officers of the naval forces, and commissioning all officers whatever in the service of the United States – making rules for the government and regulation of the said land and naval forces, and directing their operations.

The United States in Congress assembled shall have authority to appoint a committee, to sit in the recess of Congress, to be denominated "A Committee of the

States," and to consist of one delegate from each State; and to appoint such other committees and civil officers as may be necessary for managing the general affairs of the United States under their direction ;to appoint one of their members to preside, provided that no person be allowed to serve in the office of president more than one year in any term of three years; to ascertain the necessary sums of money to be raised for the service of the United States, and to appropriate and apply the same for defraying the public expenses; to borrow money, or emit bills on the credit of the United States, transmitting every half – year to the respective States an account of the sums of money so borrowed or emitted ; to build and equip a navy – to agree upon the number of land forces, and to make requisitions from each State for its quota, in proportion to the number of White inhabitants in such State; which requisition shall be binding, and thereupon the legislature of each State shall appoint the regimental officers, raise the men and clothed, arm and equip them in a soldier-like manner, at the expense of the United States; and the officers and men so clothed, armed and equipped shall march to the place appointed, and within the time agreed on by the United States in Congress assembled. But if the United States in Congress assembled shall, on consideration of circumstances judge proper that any State should not raise men, or should raise a smaller number of men than the quota thereof, such extra number shall be raised, officered, clothed, armed and quipped in the same manner as the quota of each State, unless the legislature of such State shall judge that such extra number cannot be safely spread out in the same, in which case they shall raise, officer, cloth, arm and equip as many of such extra number as they judge can be safely spared. And the officers and men so clothed, armed, and equipped, shall march to the place appointed, and

within the time agreed on by the United States in Congress assembled.

The United States in Congress assembled shall never engage in war, nor grant letters of marque or reprisal in time of peace, nor enter into any treaties or alliances, nor coin money, nor regulate the value thereof, nor ascertain the sums and expenses necessary for the defense and welfare of the United States, or any of them, nor emit bills, nor borrow money on the credit of the United States, nor appropriate money, nor agree upon the number of vessels of war, to be built or purchased, or the number of land or sea forces to be raised, nor appoint a commander in chief of the army or navy, unless nine States assent to the same: nor shall a question on any other point, except for adjourning from day to day be determined, unless by the votes of the majority of the United States in Congress assembled.

The Congress of the United States shall have power to adjourn to any time within the year, and to any place within the United States, so that no period of adjournment be for a longer duration than the space of six months, and shall publish the journal of their proceedings monthly, except such parts thereof relating to treaties, alliances or military operations, as in their judgement require secrecy; and the yeas and nays of the delegates of each State on any question shall be entered on the journal, when it is desired by any delegates of a State, or any of them, at his or their request shall be furnished with a transcript of the said journal, except such parts as are above excepted, to lay before the legislatures of the several States.

X.

The Committee of the States, or any nine of them, shall be authorized to execute, in the recess of Congress, such of the powers of Congress as the United States in Congress assembled, by the consent of the nine States, shall from time to time think expedient to vest them with; provided that no power be delegated to the said Committee, for the exercise of which, by the Articles of Confederation, the voice of nine States in the Congress of the United States Assembled be requisite.

XI.

Canada acceding to this confederation, and adjoining in the measures of the United States, shall be admitted into, and entitled to all the advantages of this Union; but no other colony shall be admitted into the same, unless such admission be agreed to by nine States.

XII.

All bill of credit emitted, monies borrowed, and debts contracted by, or under the authority of Congress, before the assembling of the United States, in pursuance of the present confederation, shall be deemed and considered as a charge against the United States, for payment and satisfaction whereof the said United States, and the public faith are hereby solemnly pledged.

XIII.

Every State shall abide by the determination of the United States in Congress assembled, on all questions which by this confederation are submitted to them. And the Articles of this Confederation shall be inviolably observed by every State, and the Union shall be perpetual; nor shall any alteration at any time hereafter be made in any of them; unless such alteration be agreed to in a Congress of the United States, and afterwards confirmed by the legislatures of every State.

And whereas it hath pleased the Great Governor of the World to incline the hearts of the legislatures we respectively represent in Congress, to approve of, and to authorize us to ratify the said Articles of Confederation and perpetual Union. Know Ye that we the undersigned delegates, by virtue of the power and authority to us given for that purpose, do by these presents, in the name and in behalf of our respective constituents, fully and entirely ratify and confirm each and every of the said Articles of Confederation and perpetual Union, and all and singular the matters and things therein contained; and we do further solemnly plight and engage the faith of our respective constituents, that they shall abide by the determinations of the United States in Congress assembled, on all questions, which by the said Confederation are submitted to them. And that the Articles thereof shall be inviolably observed by the States we respectively represent, and that the Union shall be perpetual.

In Witness whereof we have hereunto set our hand in Congress. Done at Philadelphia in the State of Pennsylvania the ninth day of July in the Year of our Lord One Thousand Seven Hundred and Seventy-Eight, and in the Third Year of the independence of America.

Agreed to by Congress 15 November 1777, In force after ratification by Maryland, 1 March 1781

* * * * *

The 13 Original Colonies were:

New Hampshire
Massachusetts
Rhode Island
Connecticut
New York
New Jersey
Pennsylvania
Delaware
Maryland
Virginia
North Carolina
South Carolina
Georgia

The Emancipation Proclamation
January 1, 1863

A Transcription
By the President of the United States of America:
A Proclamation

Whereas, on the twenty-second day of September, in the year of our Lord one thousand eight hundred and sixty-two, a proclamation was issued by the President of the United States, containing, among other things, the following, to wit:

"That on the first day of January, in the year of our Lord one thousand eight hundred and sixty-three, all persons held as slaves within any State or designated part of a State, the people whereof shall then be in rebellion against the United States, shall be then, thenceforward, and forever free; and the Executive Government of the United States, including the military and naval authority thereof, will recognize and maintain the freedom of such persons, and will do no act or acts to repress such persons, or any of them, in any efforts they may make for their actual freedom."

"That the Executive will, on the first day of January aforesaid, by proclamation, designate the States and parts of States, if nay, in which the people thereof, respectively, shall then be in rebellion against the United States; and the fact that any State, or the people thereof, shall on that day be, in good faith represented in the Congress of the United States by members chosen thereto at elections wherein a majority of the qualified voters of such State shall have participated, shall, in the absence of strong countervailing testimony, be deemed conclusive evidence that such State, and the people thereof, are not then in rebellion against the United States."

Now, therefore I, Abraham Lincoln, President of the United States, by virtue of the power in me vested as Commander-in-Chief, of the Army and Navy of the United States in time of actual armed rebellion against the authority and government of the United States, and as a fit and necessary war measure for suppressing said rebellion, do, on this first day of January, in the year of our Lord one thousand eight hundred and sixty-three, and in accordance with my purpose so to do publicly proclaimed for full period of one hundred days, from the first above mentioned, order and designate as the States and parts of States wherein the people thereof respectively, are this day in rebellion against the United States, the following, to wit:

Arkansas, Texas, Louisiana, (except the Parishes of St. Bernard, Plaquemines, Jefferson, St. John, St. Charles, St. James Ascension, Assumption, Terrebonne, Lafourche, St. Mary, St. Martin and Orleans, including the City of New Orleans) Mississippi, Alabama, Florida, Georgia, South Carolina, North Carolina, and Virginia, (except the forty-eight counties designated as West Virginia, and also the counties of Berkley, Accomac, Northampton, Elizabeth City, York, Princess Ann, and Norfolk, including the cities of Norfolk and Portsmouth), and which excepted parts, are for the present, left precisely as if this proclamation were not issued.

And by virtue of the power, and for the purpose aforesaid, I do order and declare that all persons held as slaves within said designated States, and parts of States, are, and henceforward shall be free; and that the Executive government of the United States, including the military and naval authorities thereof, will recognize and maintain the freedom of said persons.

And I hereby enjoin upon the people so declared to be free to abstain from all violence, unless in necessary self-defense; and I recommend to them that, in all cases when allowed, they labor faithfully for reasonable wages.

And I further declare and make known, that such persons of suitable condition, will be received into the armed service of the United States to garrison forts, positions, stations, and other places, and to man vessels of all sorts in said service.

And upon this act, sincerely believed to be an act of justice warranted by the Constitution, upon military necessity, I invoke the considerate judgment of mankind, and gracious favor of Almighty God.

In witness whereof, I have hereunto set my hand and caused the seal of the United States to be affixed.

Done at the City of Washington, this first day of January, in the year of our Lord one thousand eight hundred and sixty three, and of the Independence of the United States of America the eighty-seventh.

By the President : ABRAHAM LINCOLN

WILLIAM H. SEWARD, Secretary of State

The Civil Rights Act of 1866

Act of April 9, 1866

An Act to protect all Persons in the United States in their Civil Rights, and furnish the Means of their Vindication.

Be it enacted by the Senate and House of Representatives of the United States of America in Congress assembled, That all persons born in the United States and not subject to any foreign power, excluding Indians not taxed, are hereby declared to be citizens of the United States; and such citizens, of every race and color, without regard to any previous condition of slavery or involuntary servitude, except as a punishment for crime whereof the party shall have been duly convicted, shall have the same right, in every State and Territory in the United States, to make and enforce contracts, to sue, be parties, and give evidence, to inherit, purchase, lease, sell, hold, and convey real and personal property, and to full and equal benefit of all laws and proceedings for the security of person and property, as is enjoyed by White citizens, and shall be subject to like punishment, pains, and penalties, and to none other, any law, statute, ordinance, regulation, or custom, to the contrary notwithstanding.

Sec. 2. And be it further enacted, That any person who, under color of any law, statute, ordinance, regulation, or custom, shall subject, or cause to be subjected, any inhabitant of any State or Territory to the deprivation of any right secured or protected by this act, or to different punishment, pains, or penalties on account of such person having at any time been held in a condition of slavery or involuntary servitude, except as a punishment for crime whereof the party shall have been duly convicted, or by reason of his color or race, than is prescribed for the punishment of White persons, shall be deemed guilty of a misdemeanor, and, on conviction, shall be punished by fine not exceeding one thousand dollars, or imprisonment not exceeding one year, or both, in the discretion of the court.

Sec. 3. And be it further enacted, That the district courts of the United States, within their respective districts, shall have, exclusively of the courts of the several States, cognizance of all crimes and offences committed against the provisions of this act, and also, concurrently with the circuit courts of the United States, of all causes, civil and criminal, affecting persons who are denied or cannot enforce in the courts or judicial tribunals of the State or locality where they may be any of the rights secured to them by the first section of this act; and if any suit or prosecution, civil or criminal, has been or shall be commenced in any State court, against any such person, for any cause whatsoever, or against any officer, civil or military, or other person, for any arrest or imprisonment, trespasses, or wrongs done or committed by virtue or under color of authority derived from this act or the act establishing a Bureau for the relief of Freedmen and Refugees, and all acts amendatory thereof, or for refusing to do any act upon the ground that it would be inconsistent with this act, such defendant shall have the right to remove such cause for trial to the proper district or circuit court in the manner prescribed by the "Act relating to habeas corpus and regulating judicial proceedings in certain cases," approved March three, eighteen hundred and sixty-three, and all act amendatory thereof. The jurisdiction in civil and criminal matters hereby conferred on the district and circuit courts of the United States shall be exercised and enforced in conformity with the laws of the United States, so far as such laws are suitable to carry the same into effect; but all cases where such laws are not adapted to the object, or are deficient in the provisions necessary to furnish suitable remedies and punish offences against law, the common law, as modified and changed by the constitution and statutes of the State wherein the court having jurisdiction of the cause, civil or criminal, is held, so far as the same is not inconsistent with the Constitution and laws of the United States, shall be extended to and govern said courts in the trial and disposition of such cause, and if of a criminal nature, in the infliction of punishment on the party found guilty.

Sec. 4. And be it further enacted. That the district attorneys, marshals, and deputy marshals of the United States, the commissioners appointed by the circuit and territorial courts of the United States with powers of arresting, imprisoning, or bailing offenders against the laws of the United States, the officers and agents of the Freedmen's Bureau, and every other officer who may be specially empowered by the President of the United States, shall be, and they are hereby, specially authorized and required, at the expense of the United States, to institute proceedings against all and every person who shall violate the provisions of this act, and cause him or them to be arrested and imprisoned, or bailed, as the case may be, for trial before such court of the United States or territorial court as by this act has cognizance of the offence. And with a view to affording reasonable protection to all persons in their constitutional rights of equality before the law, without distinction of race or color, or previous condition of slavery or involuntary servitude, except as punishment for crime, whereof the party shall have been dully convicted, and the prompt discharge of the duties of this act, it shall be the duty of the circuit courts of the United States and the superior courts of the Territories of the United States, from time to time, to increase the number of commissioners, so as to afford a speedy and convenient means for the arrest and examination of persons charged with violation of this act; and such commissioners are hereby authorized and required to exercise and discharge all the powers and duties conferred on them by this act, and the same duties with regard to offences created by this act, as they are authorized by law to exercise with regard to other offences against the laws of the United States.

Sec. 5. And be it further enacted, That it shall be the duty of all marshal and deputy marshals to obey and execute all warrants and precepts issued under the provisions of this act, when to them directed; and should any marshal or deputy marshal refuse to receive such warrant or other process when tendered, or to sue all proper means diligently to execute the same, he shall, on conviction thereof, be fined in the sum of one thousand dollars, to the use of the person upon whom the accused is alleged to have committed the offence. And the better to enable the said commissioners to execute their duties faithfully and efficiently, in conformity with the Constitution of the United States and requirements of this act, they are hereby authorized and empowered, within their counties respectively, to appoint, in writing, under their hands, any one or more suitable persons, from time to time, to execute all such warrants and other process as my be issued by them in the lawful performance of their respective duties; and the persons so appointed to execute any warrant of process as aforesaid shall have authority to summon and call to their aid the bystanders or posse comitatus of the proper county, or such portion of the land or naval forces of the United States, or the militia, as may be necessary to the performance of the duty with which they are charged, and to insure a faithful observance of the clause of the Constitution which prohibits slavery, in conformity with the provisions of this act; and said warrants shall run an be executed by said officers anywhere in the State or Territory within which they are issued.

Sec. 6. And be it further enacted, That any person who shall knowingly and willfully obstruct, hinder, or prevent any officer, or other person charged with the execution of any warrant or process issued under the provisions of this act, or any person or persons lawfully assisting him or them, from arresting any person for whose apprehension such warrant or process may have been issued, or shall rescue or attempt to rescue such person from the custody of the officer, other person or persons, or those lawfully assisting as aforesaid, when so arrested pursuant to the authority herein given and declared, or shall aid, abet, or assist any person so arrested as aforesaid, directly or indirectly, to escape from the custody of the officer or other person legally authorized as aforesaid, or shall harbor or conceal any person for whose arrest a warrant or process shall have been issued as aforesaid, so as to prevent his discovery and arrest after notice or knowledge of the fact that a warrant has been issued for the apprehension of such personal, shall, for either of said offences, be subject to fine not exceeding one thousand dollars, and imprisonment not exceeding six months, by indictment and conviction before the district court of the United States for the district in which said offence may have been committed, or before the proper court of criminal jurisdiction, if committed within any one of the organized Territories of the United States.

Sec. 7. And be it further enacted, That the district attorneys, the marshals, their deputies, and the clerks of the said district and territorial courts shall be paid for their services the like fees as may be allowed to them for similar services in other cases; and in all cases where the proceedings are before a commissioner, he shall be entitled to a fee of ten dollars in full for his services in each case, inclusive of all services incident to such arrest and examination. The person or persons authorized to execute the process to be issued by such commissioners for the arrest of offenders against the provisions of this act shall be entitled to a fee of five dollars for each person he or they may arrest and take before any such commissioner as aforesaid, with such other fees as may be deemed reasonable by such commissioner for such other additional services as may be necessarily performed by him or them, such as attending at the examination, keeping the prisoner in custody, and providing him with food and lodging during his detention, and until the final determination of

Such commissioner, and in general for performing such other duties as may be required in the premises; such fees to be made up in conformity with the fees usually charged by the officers of the courts of justice within the proper district or county, as near as may be practicable, and paid out of the Treasury of the United States on the certificated of the judge of the district within which the arrest is made, and to be recoverable from the defendant as part of the judgment in case of conviction.

Sec. 8. And be it further enacted, That whenever the President of the United States shall have reason to believe that offences have been or are likely to be committed against the provisions of this act within any judicial district, it shall be lawful for him, in his discretion, to direct the judge, marshal, and district attorney of such district to attend at such place within the district, and for such time as he may designate, for the purpose of the more speedy arrest and trial of persons charged with a violation of this act; and it shall be the duty of every judge or other officer, when any such requisition shall be received by him, to attend at the place and for the time therein designated.

Sec. 9. And be it further enacted, That it shall be lawful for the President of the United States, or such person as he may empower for that purpose, to employ such part of the land or naval forces of the United States, or of the militia, as shall be necessary to prevent the violation and enforce the due execution of this act.

Sec. 10. And be it further enacted, That upon all questions of law arising in any cause under the provisions of this act a final appeal my be taken to the Supreme Court of the United States.

Speaker of the House of Representatives.
La Fayette S. Foster,
President of the Senate, Pro Tempore.

In the Senate of the United States, April 6, 1866

The President of the United States having returned to the Senate, in which it originated, the bill entitled "An act to protect all persons in the United States in their civil rights, and furnish the means of their vindication," with his objections thereto, the Senate proceeded, in pursuance of the Constitution, to reconsider the same; and,

Resolved, That the said bill do pass, two-thirds of the Senate agreeing to pass the same.

Attest: J.W. Forney,
Secretary of the Senate
In the House of Representatives U.S.
April 9th, 1866

The House of Representative having proceeded, in pursuance of the Constitution, to reconsider the bill entitled "An act to protect all persons in the United States in their civil rights, and furnish the means of their vindication," returned to the Senate by the President of the United States, with his objections, and sent by the Senate to the House of Representatives, with the message of the President returning the bill:

Resolved, That the bill do pass, two-thirds of the House of Representatives agreeing to pass the same.

Attest: Edward McPherson, Clerk
by, Clinton Lloyd, Chief Clerk

* * * * *

Note:

In 1883, the U.S. Supreme Court began to strike down the foundations of the post-Civil War Reconstruction, declaring the Civil Rights Act unconstitutional. The Court also ruled that the Fourteenth Amendment prohibited state governments from discriminating against people because of race, but did not restrict private organizations or individuals from doing so. Thus railroads, hotels, theaters, and the like could legally practice segregation. It is interesting how people in power change and interpret the laws according to their needs and wants.

* * * * *

Another CIVIL RIGHTS ACT was passed by the Senate and House of Representatives of the United States of America in Congress assembled, this Act may be cited as the "Civil Rights Act of 1964."

Read the Act of 1964 at:

AFRO-AMERICAN ALMANAC
www.toptags.com/aama/docs/act1964.html

* * * * *

United States Constitution

Since the U.S. Constitution is very long, we have only included Amendments, 13, 14 & 15, those that specially pertain to Blacks, slaves and involuntary servitudes.

AMENDMENT 13 (ratified Dec. 6, 1865)

Section 1. Neither slavery nor involuntary servitude, except as a punishment for crime whereof the party shall have been duly convicted, shall exist within the United States, or any place subject to their jurisdiction.

AMENDMENT 14 (ratified July 9,1868)

Section 1. All persons born or naturalized in the United States, and subject to the jurisdiction on thereof, are citizens of the United States and of the State wherein they reside. No State shall make or enforce any law which abridge the privileges or immunities of citizens of the United States; nor shall any State deprive any person of life, liberty, or property, without due process of law; nor deny to any person within its jurisdiction the equal protection of the laws.

AMENDMENT 15 (ratified February 3, 1870)

Section 1. The right of citizens of the United States to vote shall not be denied or abridged by the United States or by any State on account of race, color, or previous condition of servitude.

Constitution of the Confederate States
(As It Related To Slaves)

ARTICLE I Section IX.

No. 1. The importation of Negroes of the African race from any foreign country other than the slaveholding States or Territories of the United States of America, is hereby forbidden; and Congress is required to pass such laws as shall effectually prevent the same.

No 2. Congress shall also have power to prohibit the introduction of slaves from any State not a member of or Territory not belonging to this Confederacy.

No. 3. No bill of attainder, ex post facto law, or law denying or impairing the right of property in Negro slaves shall be passed.

ARTICLE IV.

Section I.

No. 1 The citizen of each State shall be entitled to all the privileges and immunities of citizens in the several States; and shall have the right of transit and sojourn in any State of this Confederacy, with their Slaves and other property; and the right of property in said slaves shall not be thereby impaired.

No. 2. No slave or other person held to service or labor in a State or Territory of the Confederate States, under the laws thereof, escaping or lawfully carried into another, shall, in consequence of any law or regulation therein, be discharged from such service or labor; but shall be delivered up on claim of the party to whom such slave belongs; or whom such service or labor may be due.

Section II.

No. 1. The Confederate States may acquire new territory; and Congress shall have power to legislate and provide governments for the inhabitants of all territory belonging to the Confederate States, lying without the limits of the several States; and may permit them at such times, and in such manner as it may by law provide, to form States to be admitted into the Confederacy. In all such territory the institution of negro slavery, as it now exists in the Confederate States, shall be recognized and protected by Congress and by the Territorial government; and the inhabitants of the several Confederate States and Territories shall have the right to take to such Territory any slaves lawfully held by them in any of the States or Territories of the Confederate States.

* * * * *

LIST OF SOURCES

Allen, James, Als, Shelton, Lewis, John, Congressman, Litwack, Leon F.
"WITHOUT SANCTUARY"
Publisher: Twin Palms Publishing, 2000
P.O. Box 10229
Santa Fe, NM 87504-1022

Anderson, Claude, Ph.D.
"DIRTY LITTLE SECRETS"
Publisher: Power Nomics Corp. of America
P.O. Box 30536
Bethesda, MD 20814

Andreas, Joel
"ADDICTED TO WAR"
Publisher: Frank Dorrel
P.O. Box 3261
Culver City, CA 90231-3261

BaKhufu, Dr. Auset
"THE SIX BLACK PRESIDENTS: BLACK BLOOD, WHITE MASKS - USA"
Publisher: PIK^2 Publications, 1993
% A & A Distributors
P.O. Box 1113 –AA
Temple Hill, MD 20757

Burt Jr., McKinley,
"BLACK INVENTORS OF AMERICA,"
Publisher: National Book Company, 1969
Portland, OR

Cleage Jr., Albert B
"THE BLACK MESSIAH"
Publisher: Africa World Press, Inc., 1989
P.O. Box 1892
Trenton, NJ 08607

Cowan, Tom, Ph.D and Maguire, Jack
"TIMELINE OF AFRICAN-AMERICAN HISTORY"
Publisher: The Berkley Publishing Group, 1994
New York

Ginzburg, Ralph
"100 YEARS OF LYNCHING"

Harris, Middleton, with the assistance of
Levitt, Morris, Furman, Roger, Smith, Ernest
"THE BLACK BOOK"
Publisher: Random House, Inc.
1745 Broadway
New York, NY 10019

Jackson, John G.
"ETHIOPIA AND THE ORIGIN OF CIVILIZATION"
Publisher: Black Classic Press %, 1980
List
P.O. Box 13414
Baltimore, MD 21203

James, George G.M.
"STOLEN LEGACY"
Publisher:
United Brothers Communications Systems, 1954
P.O. Box 5368
Newport News, VA 23605

Kush, Indus Knamit
"WHAT THEY NEVER TOLD YOU IN HISTORY CLASS"
Publisher: Luxorr Publications, 1983
405 West 49th Street, #30
New York, NY 10019-7233

Mosley, William
"WHAT COLOR WAS JESUS?"
Publisher: African American Images, 1987
1909 West 95th Street
Chicago, IL 60643

Rogers, J.A.
"100 AMAZING FACTS ABOUT THE NEGRO"
Publisher: Helga M. Rogers, 1957
4975 59th Avenue South
St. Petersburg, FL 33715

Rogers, J.A.
"FIVE NEGRO PRESIDENTS"
Publisher: Helga M. Rogers, 1965
4975 59th Avenue South
St. Petersburg, FL 33715

Rogers, J.A.
"NATURE KNOWS NO COLOR LINE"
Publisher: Helga M. Rogers, 1952
4975 59th Avenue South
St. Petersburg, FL 33715

Rogers, J.A.
"SEX AND RACE, VOL. 1, 2, & 3"
Publisher: Helga M. Rogers, 1942, 1944
4975 59th Avenue South
St. Petersburg, FL 33715

Shabaka, Negest Shaba with Smith, Dr. Ernie A.
"NIGGER, A DIVINE ORIGIN"
Publisher: Shabban Publishers, Inc.
P.O. Box 11765
Los Angeles, CA 90011

Shabaka, Negest Shaba
"NIGRITIA, AN INTRODUCTION"
Publisher: Shabban Publishers, Inc., 1992
P.O. Box 11765
Los Angeles, CA 90011

Vaughn, Leroy William, M.D. M.B.A.
"BLACK PEOPLE & THEIR PLACE IN WORLD HISTORY"
Publisher: Dr. Leroy William Vaughn, 2002
323 North Prairie Ave. Suite 217
Inglewood, CA 90301

Williams, Dr. Chancellor
"THE DESTRUCTION OF BLACK CIVILIZATION"
Publisher: Third World Press, 1976
7524 S. Cottage Grove Avenue
Chicago, IL 60619

Windsor, Rudolph R.
"FROM BABYLON TO TIMBUKTU"
Publisher: Windsor's Golden Series, 1988
P.O. Box 310393
Atlanta, GA 30331

Windsor, Rudolph R.
"VALLEY OF THE DRY BONES"
Publisher: Windsor's Golden Series, 1988
P.O. Box 310393
Atlanta, GA 30331

Woodson, Carter G.
"THE MIS-EDUCATION OF THE NEGRO"
Publisher: African World Press, Inc., 1933

* * * * *

FINISH STRONG

IT'S NOT AS IMPORTANT WHERE
YOU START OFF IN LIFE, BUT WHERE YOU FINISH.
THERE ARE THOSE THAT START OFF STRONG,
ONLY TO DROP IN THE LONG RUN.
THERE ARE THOSE THAT START OFF SLOW OR LATE,
BUT FINISH STRONG.
KEEP YOUR COURSE, IT'S NEVER TOO LATE

By Dr. Romeo L. Taylor, Sr.

LIST OF SOURCES FOR PHOTOGRAPHS AND PICTURES

Notes